The Barefoot Investor

The Barefoot Investor

Five steps to financial freedom in your 20s and 30s

Scott Pape

Adapted by Peter Temple

CAPSTONE

Published in 2006 by   Capstone Publishing Ltd (A Wiley Company) The Atrium,
                           Southern Gate, Chichester, West Sussex, PO19 8SQ, England
                           Phone (+44) 1243 779777

Copyright © 2006   Scott Pape

Published by arrangement with Pluto Press Australia, Victoria, Australia

Email (for orders and customer service enquires): cs-books@wiley.co.uk
Visit our Home Page on www.wiley.co.uk or www.wiley.com

This publication is designed to provide accurate and authoritative information in regard to the
subject matter covered. It is sold on the understanding that the Publisher is not engaged in
rendering professional services. If professional advice or other expert assistance is required,
the services of a competent professional should be sought.

Scott Pape has asserted his right under the Copyright, Designs and Patents Act 1988, to be
identified as the author of this work.

Other Wiley Editorial Offices

John Wiley & Sons, Inc. 111 River Street, Hoboken, NJ 07030, USA

Jossey-Bass, 989 Market Street, San Francisco, CA 94103-1741, USA

Wiley-VCH Verlag GmbH, Pappellaee 3, D-69469 Weinheim, Germany

John Wiley & Sons Australia, Ltd, 33 Park Road, Milton, Queensland, 4064, Australia

John Wiley & Sons (Asia) Pte Ltd, 2 Clementi Loop #02-01, Jin Xing Distripark, Singapore
129809

John Wiley & Sons Canada Ltd, 22 Worcester Road, Etobicoke, Ontario, Canada, M9W 1L1

Wiley also publishes its books in a variety of electronic formats. Some content that appears in
print may not be available in electronic books.

British Library Cataloguing in Publication Data

A catalogue record for this book is available from the British Library
ISBN-13   978-1-84112-715-6 (HB)
ISBN-10   1-84112-715-9 (HB)

Typeset in 11/15pt Optima by MCS Publishing Services Ltd, Salisbury, Wiltshire.
Printed and bound in Great Britain by T.J. International, Padstow, Cornwall.
This book is printed on acid-free paper responsibly manufactured from sustainable forestry in
which at least two trees are planted for each one used for paper production.
10 9 8 7 6 5 4 3 2

Dedicated to my family – the most important people in my life

Contents

Acknowledgments

The *Barefoot Investor* started as a radio program and Kane Munro helped get it to air faultlessly, special thanks to Kane as producer, coach, adviser and friend. Without Kane's support and guidance I'm not sure Barefoot would have made it this far. Thanks too, to Sophie Garland my co-host, and all the guests that have appeared on the show. Special thanks also to all at Pluto Press who spearheaded *The Barefoot Investor* book project and had the guts to take on something that was different.

Along the way many people have provided assistance and support. They include: the Barefoot Entrepreneurs profiled, Natalie Bloom and Peter Alexander, who gave their time so freely and allowed me a peels into their inspiring lives; Jodie Burns who taught me what family is all about; Martin King for his kind words; Sir Richard Branson for his kind words; Neil Jenman for being one of the few people to tell it to me straight; Sue Byrne and Robert Dungey for giving me my start in the wonderful world of stockbroking and my colleagues at Baillieu Stockbroking Limited for putting up with me. Also Matt Symes and Ross Smith, two of my oldest and dearest friends who truly are treading their own paths; Tom Robertson my travel companion, gym buddy, all round top bloke and great friend;

Eliza Dwyer, thanks for everything you've done – you're the best person I know, Tye Everett for teaching me so many things; Katherine Parry for 'keeping it real'; James Eckersley (aka the Checkman) – Checkers you're one of the few truly cool people out there, thanks for teaching me about what matters most.

To the Timcke's – thanks so much for your love and support, for believing in everything I do, and for giving me something to aspire to. Angus and Sam this book has been written with you in mind, you're both Barefooters before you've uttered a word. Terry Boucher (aka Mr Magoo) – thanks for the long chats over lattes, I've learnt a lot (even if I am still the apprentice). James Tamanika of JAM thanks for the marketing advice. Jim Buckell – editor, chef and friend, without your help this project would never have taken shape, thanks for taking the time to teach me. Melissa Law, you've always been there and always will be.

A big thank you from the bottom of my heart to my family, especially Mum and Dad who are the greatest supporters and friends I could ever ask for. Last but not least, thank you to Alan Wilson. Al, most of the time we're on different wavelengths, yet I admire the qualities that make you one of the most caring people in my life – thanks for giving me the time, space and support which has allowed me to embark on this journey, I'm forever grateful.

Scott Pape, September 2004

Going Barefoot

There's a Barefoot Path for everyone

Most teenagers rebel. Some do it by cutting school or getting tattoos while others hide in their rooms and listen to Nirvana.

I rebelled against the institutions that I was a by-product of – middle class suburbia, and an educational system that was designed to perpetuate the same myopia. I had no desire to become part of the rat race.

Throughout my school years, success had been presented as an easily digestible modus operandi: 'Study hard, get a good job, and be set for life'. I started to question this truth after having it screamed at me by a middle-aged maths teacher who looked as though he'd done one too many rounds of playground duty – he was a successful graduate of the same three-step formula.

My teenage angst led me to search for an alternative path – a Barefoot Path, that would allow me to do the things that I wanted without getting caught in the trap of working my arse off to pay for stuff that I really didn't need in the first place.

My rebellion wasn't about dying my hair, having an Eminem-esque attitude, or binge drinking (well, maybe just a little), but more about how I could use money as a tool to bypass the pervading culture. Money meant one thing to me: freedom. The freedom to do the things that I wanted to do. Freedom from the rat race.

I've been fortunate to have many positive influences in my life, from wise old stockbrokers who tools me under their wing, and my parents who fanned the flames of my economic interests, which was fortunate, given that in my thirteen years of schooling I was never once taught about money.

Early on I decided that the flight to my future life wasn't going to be travelled in economy class. I devised a strategy that would allow me to tread my own path, afford me the choices about how I would work and live now and in the future, and never have to worry about money again.

Reality check

Advertising has us chasing cars and clothes, working jobs we hate so we can buy shit we don't need. We've all been raised on television to believe that one day we'd all be millionaires, and movie gods, and rock stars. But we won't. And we're slowly learning that fact. And we're very, very pissed off.
TYLER DURDEN (PLAYED BY BRAD PITT), *FIGHT CLUB*

I went to university, experimented, partied, played, studied, and came out the other end with a business card that read Scott Pape, graduate trainee, a desk in a skyscraper and a coffee mug that had my name on it – not that it mattered. I had a plan. *A Barefoot Plan.*

Many of my friends also finished university and graduated to positions that brought with them below average salaries, mounting bills (and the accompanying mounting debt) and work hours that went some way to curbing their appetite for 5 am finishes. They had fulfilled their end of the success formula (letters after their name, good job) – it was now time to be 'set for life'.

Just like learning about computers on an original Apple Mac, much of what I learned through high school later became redundant. Thirty years ago when it seemed the only people who went to university were hippies trying to get out of going to the Vietnam War, higher education (funded by the government) was probably the next best thing to joining the Mafia.

Today things have changed. The bar has been raised. My generation is the best educated in history – as a consequence we're all competing for the same jobs. These days a graduate degree will see you on the fast track to be junior vice president of burger flipping and cost you thousands of pounds in student loans.

House prices have gone through the roof. Young people are squeezed out of the market, or burdened with mortgages that could wipe out the debt of a Third World country. Masses of Baby Boomers congratulate themselves on being shrewd investors as they see the value of their house going up, up, up, while those faithful to the three-step track to success sit on the sidelines paying rent.

Many of my friends felt cheated – the financial cards were stacked against them. As they struggled to get by their thoughts weren't focused on which house, car or holiday to purchase, but on how to pay their bills.

Not me. I'm a guy who has money.

I don't clip coupons, I eat out, I spend money on CDs, concerts, travel, and a host of other things that add value to my life. Invariably my friends would come to me and ask what I was doing differently (since we were all on roughly the same money).

I explain that the source of my success doesn't lie in a huge salary, living like an Amish convert surviving on a dollar a day, or even on disciplined budgeting (I've never stuck to one successfully for longer than a few days). Nor was it about being a financial wizard malting a killing on the stock market. The difference between me and my friends was that I had a plan. A Barefoot Plan.

The Barefoot Plan has evolved into a series of steps that can be implemented within the space of an afternoon and require no more additional thought than it takes to watch an episode of *Big Brother*. It doesn't require a huge income, an interest in investing or keen analytical skills, and takes only a tiny dose of willpower or determination.

I don't pretend that I know your goals. You're an individual. Your goals will invariably cost money, be it buying a house, travelling, or starting your own business. The Barefoot Plan sets you on course not only to become wealthy beyond what you've ever envisioned, but more importantly it gives you the ability to tread your own unique path in life, experiencing life on your terms – something that will mean much more to you than money.

What does the Barefoot Investor stand for?

There is only one success — to be able to spend your life in your own way
CHRISTOPHER MORLEY

I like money – so much so that I have written a book about it. Money is a very serious topic. Most people would agree that when you talk about money you don't want advice from someone without the requisite grey hair – much less someone under the age of thirty.

So, I hear you ask, who am I to be telling you how to sort out your finances? Let me say from the outset who I'm not. For a start, I'm not your traditional investment man, I'm not your high school economics teacher, I'm not even Evan Davies on the BBC News. My name is Scott Pape, I'm twenty-six, I'm a stockbroker in Australia and I run my own radio talk show called *The Barefoot Investor*.

I started *The Barefoot Investor* with the aim of teaching personal finance in a different way to anything – or anyone – that has come before it. I'm well aware that the media may pigeonhole this book as a 'young person's guide to finance', but I've never been overly focused on targeting a certain age group. I've focused on delivering relevant, effective advice for people of any age, and made the process of learning about it a hell of a lot of fun.

You'll quickly see that this isn't your typical run-of-the-mill 'charts and figures' personal finance book. If that's all I could offer I wouldn't have bothered with the arduous task of writing a book. After all, bookshops are already overrun with titles teaching you about money.

My radio program, *The Barefoot Investor*, has been described as finance for people who don't 'do' finance – which is easily the best compliment I've ever received. With this thought in mind I've written this book in much the same fashion.

For most people, if they were faced with the choice of either reading a 'money book' or Liam Gallager's autobiography, they'd probably choose the Oasis star's story – and I couldn't agree more.

Most finance books are written by, and aimed at, people older (and wealthier) than me. When I first set out to learn about finance, most of what I read was relentlessly boring. It simply didn't cut it. The essence of personal finance is about helping you to achieve the things that are most important to you – which, goddamn it, is downright sexy!

The Barefoot Investor is all about taking a different view of finance and how it relates to us. We've had it rammed down our throats by middle-aged men in cheap suits that investing is a serious and complicated process.

Why should it be that way?

The Barefoot Investor is more than a catchy title. It's about learning about money and using it in a way that brings you the most pleasure. It can be fun, exciting and about as complicated as a Year 8 home economics class.

I really don't care for accumulating money for money's sake. I'm not sexually stimulated by the sight of fresh wads of hundred-dollar notes – and hopefully you're not either.

The premise behind *The Barefoot Investor is* not focused on being greedy – accumulating money for money's sake nor is it about reducing the fun you have now so that you can enjoy your golden years. If you're like me, the thought of living like a leper while you're in the prime of your life just so that you can live comfortably when you're bald and have none of your original teeth left and your idea of fun is watching *Antiques Roadshow* seems like a pretty stupid payoff.

It's not about being yuppie scum, talking to your stockbroker on your brand new Nokia while sipping a cafe latte. It's not about being the richest person on the block, hoarding your money till you're sixty-five, or scrimping over a 99p bargan. It's about working out what you want from this thing we call life and using your assets (all of them) in order to get you there.

For some it could be a once in a lifetime holiday backpacking across America. For others it may be buying a house in the burbs with a white picket fence. It doesn't matter. What matters is that you learn to allocate your money away from stupid stuff that has little or no effect on your life, towards things that will make a real difference to you.

Once your financial house is in order you will experience a new sense of freedom, which is ultimately what we all want. Freedom to live and experience life in any way we choose fit, which, when all is said and done, is what finance is really all about.

The way of the Barefooter

The Barefoot Investor could be crudely described as a money show, in that on the radio program we talk about investing, saving, and spending your hard-earned cash, but there's more to it than that.

The thing that differentiates us from other finance jocks is our underlying approach to the role that money plays in our lives. The size of your bank account is not a prerequisite to your happiness – I strongly believe that money is quite simply a medium of exchange that allows us to live a life with choices.

It seems that most people have screwed-up ideas about money.

There are some people who think that if they were rich then their life would be complete. It's a fairly common assumption – after all, who doesn't want more money? Yet from personal experience working in the world of high finance and dealing with people who have large amounts of money, I can categorically state that there are just as many miserable and stressed-out people among the wealthy as there are among the poor.

It's often been said that money acts like a magnifier. If you're unhappy when you're poor, coming into cash will tend to magnify those feelings. If you're happy with your lot and you get a windfall, research tends to indicate that you'll be a happy rich person. For validation of this point, just check out any of those trashy magazines that dish the dirt on the rich and famous. It's clear that some of these people, despite their wealth, fame and adulation, battle with depression. Think Britney Spears and weddings, Courtney Love and white powder, or Michael Jackson and children.

Many people say that money is 'the root of all evil'. I don't buy that at all. The underlying philosophy of the Barefoot Investor is that money is not inherently evil, at least, not like Brian May's hair is inherently evil; it's simply a means to an end.

The real deal is that being responsible about the choices you make regarding the money you earn (and later invest) allows you freedom of choice. With money in your hip pocket you call the shots. Money allows you to be in control of your career – or lack of one. You can donate your time to something you're passionate about. You can follow your calling, live your dreams, tread your own path.

So while it's true that money is an important part of people's lives, and something that creates a considerable amount of stress, by implementing effective strategies, and directing your money towards the things that mean the most to you, you can live a unique and prosperous life.

I am able to live the way that I want right now because I make choices about how I want to live, and then direct my time, energy and financial resources to getting to that point. Sure, I may not be living the Country Life catalogue lifestyle, I don't have a car that costs more than the GDP of some developing nations and my clothes aren't designer label, but at the end of the day I simply couldn't give a toss.

I don't care about buying into the status symbol game. I have true peace of mind, and the ability to do the things that mean the most to me. Get your finances in order and you'll be able to do the same.

Money to me is not about conforming to the ideals of my family, friends, co-workers, or of marketing people. I have money, and the overriding factor that gets me jazzed is not the Gucci shoes I could splash my cash on, it's true freedom – freedom of choice.

At the tender age of twenty-six I have freedom of choice. I choose to do the things that mean something to me. Huh? Let's break it down.

For about the last seven years I lived in that unique quasi 'family environment' that is the flat share. All up I'd say I've lived in maybe ten different addresses across the country. As much as I've tried, my living arrangements are more *He Died with a Felafel in His Hand* than *The Secret Life of Us*.

I've lived in colleges at university that made *Animal House* look like *Jackanory*. I've shared houses with guys who model themselves on the likes of Charlie Sheen and Robert Downey Jnr. I've put up with dodgy stuff happening in the bathroom, landlords threatening to kill me, roommates stealing my food, having to watch *Trinny and Susanna* instead of *Match of the Day* because the girls got there first. I've had real estate agents putting a 'hit' on me, surprise inspections, lack of privacy, and I've dealt with the trials and tribulations of other moody twentysomethings. After seven years I got to the end of my tether. I couldn't handle it anymore.

Because I'm responsible with the cash that I earn, and I've managed to keep my overheads low, I made the decision that it was time for me to get my own Barefoot pad. So because of this, I'm sitting here on my uber-cool bouncy ball, tapping away on my laptop, listening to the melodic tunes of the Beastie Boys in my very own studio apartment.

Money gives you choices. It gives you peace of mind. It allows you to live the life you want. Forget those less enlightened that denounce money as evil. It's a tool, and how you use it depends on your ideals, your character and, importantly, your goals.

The Barefoot Plan for living large in five easy steps

The Barefoot Plan is delivered in five separate steps. Each step builds upon the last and will culminate in delivering your personal version of the Barefoot Plan that will allow you to easily achieve the goals that mean the most to you.

- **STEP 1: Keep it real**

- **STEP 2: Look out for number one**

- **STEP 3: Repo your repayments**

- **STEP 4: Work your mojo**

- **STEP 5: Have a backup plan**

I've designed this book differently to most traditional finance texts. I don't presuppose there is one correct path that we should all be striving towards; I won't be giving cookie cutter advice on how to save by clipping coupons, or lecture you about spending money on nights out with your friends (that's something I actually encourage).

I have taught this plan to hundreds of people, on my radio show, in personal consultation and to some of my closest friends. Each person had different income levels – some were outrageously wealthy, others were on income support, some had costly goals like travelling first class overseas or buying a house, others simply wanted to get out of debt. All of them wanted to gain control over their finances so they could start living a life unconstrained by lack of money. The results people have achieved with the Barefoot Plan never ceases to amaze me.

From reading my introduction you'll hopefully have gleaned that I don't write like other finance writers. I have no interest in boring you with complicated lingo that serves nothing but to stroke my ego. Nor am I attempting to go off on a tangent and waffle on about irrelevant financial facts.

In the Introduction I promised that:

• Formulating your own Barefoot Plan would take the best part of an afternoon, and after it's in place you won't need to spend another second thinking about it.

• The plan requires no great sacrifices, or cutting back on the pleasures of life, and little in the way of budgeting (just bondage, but more on that later).

• You don't need to have any interest in money, except for an interest in where you want to spend it.

• You require no financial knowledge.

• I would provide you with a road map that will deliver you riches, peace of mind and the ability to tread your own path.

1

Keep it Real

BAREFOOT STEP 1

Let's get this party started. In the first chapter we're going to tackle:

- Figuring out how much it costs to live (without joining a convent).
- The issues that people face in building wealth in the new millennium.
- The Barefoot approach to living an authentic life.
- Cutting through the lifestyle marketing propaganda.
- My tour of duty delivers me some perspective.

• Finding your own unique path in life. Identifying the things that are most important to you.

We'll also spend time creating the fuel to fire your own unique Barefoot Plan.

The label game

My first day of high school feels like it was yesterday.

I was thirteen, and seriously stressed about leaving the confines of my little primary school to jump into the land where the big kids ruled. Adding to my angst was the fact that the high school had deemed our first day to be 'non-uniform day' for the whole school, as a 'special treat' to welcome the new boys to the school.

'Special treat my arse!' I remember thinking to myself. I secretly wished that the first day could be full school uniform, at least then everyone would look the same. Alas, not only was the new Year Seven class thrown into the deep end having to deal with all the new surroundings, damn it we had to look cool too!

The day before I remember scrounging through my wardrobe desperately searching for something passable.

Nope, nada, nothing. That's what you get for letting your mother buy clothes for you for the first thirteen years of your life, and relying on family hand-me-downs to suffice. But hey, I was thirteen, what did I know about fashion? At this stage I was in a sheer state of panic. What would happen to me if I turned up wearing stuff that wasn't cool? Would they think I was a mummy's boy?

The fear was driving me insane. Taking the money I had saved from my paper round, I mosied down to the local shopping centre and pleaded mercy with a shop assistant to deck me out in something cool for my first day of high school.

At the time, Gap was *the* label. Back then, in the early 90s, brand names were yet to encounter the backlash that they have now. For most of us, it didn't really matter what you wore so long as it had some god-awful brand label stuck on it – the more prominent and expensive, the better.

So after using all my spare cash, I was the proud owner of a pair of Gap shorts and a (hideous) Gap T-shirt. It mattered not that if these items of clothing didn't have the Gap emblem I wouldn't be caught dead in them, at least I wouldn't stand out, and I'd pass the test in the nervous few hours of starting a new school.

The next day as I neared the school gates I noticed a funny thing – practically every fresher had the same idea. You could pick the new kids a mile off, each piece of clothing had come freshly off the retail rack the day before and had been ironed within an inch of its life.

Cut to adulthood: do you think the issue of conforming and appearing with the right material possessions has changed? God no. If anything, as you move through your turbulent teen years and towards the process of sitting at the adults' table the pressure gets worse.

In the groundbreaking book *Greed Is Good: The Capitalist Pig Guide to Investing*, author Jonathan Hoenig details the extent of lifestyle based marketing and the effect of what he calls the 'selling of imagery' on young American consumers.

Everywhere, people are bombarded by marketing, which tells us that if we purchase certain clothes it will make us more attractive, that the car we drive is directly related to our sex appeal, and that true happiness can be found in a catalogue.

Greed is good?

I've literally read hundreds of books on finance, some good, some average, and some that were complete crap. **Greed is Good: The Capitalist Pig Guide to Investing** by Jonathan Hoenig (HarperCollins), is one of the few great books on the often dry subject of money. Check it out.

Society dictates to us what success is, and this is highly influenced by the marketing hype that bombards us. The deal apparently is this: you will be happy, successful, fulfilled and loved if you have the requisite status symbols, be it the type of car you drive, a piece of clothing with a designer label that's difficult to pronounce, a clock on your arm, a house in the right suburb, yada, yada, yada.

I don't want to make money. I just want to be wonderful

MARILYN MONROE

Television has a major impact on society, and consequently plays a role in influencing our expectations of what our lives should look like. You see the lifestyles that the characters on your favourite sitcoms are living and feel depressed. On the face of it, we all know that television is fantasyland, but that's not to say that our sub-conscious minds see the images flickering away on the TV and somehow associate this with something close to reality.

This is not how people go about their everyday lives. Have you ever noticed how the characters on your favourite show spend very little time watching television?

A report came out some time a go that said that if the funky group of thirtysomethings on the show *Friends* were to live the lifestyle of the hip and funky New Yorkers that they portray on the show, each of the characters would have to be earning well over $US100 000 a year!

Now in between all the high jinks, and coffee lounging that happens, my bet is that there's not much time left over to bring home the bacon, unless of course Chandler is running a downtown amphetamine ring and supplying the rest of them with the cash to support their lifestyles.

Get married, have 2.3 children, wear the Country Casual garb, shop at Harvey Nichols and drive a Beamer. Then you'll be happy. Then you won't have a worry in the world. It's a game, its unrealistic, generic and plastic.

My personal experience of working in the fast-paced world of stock-broking has confirmed that people still happily eat this garbage up. Throughout my career I've worked with guys who, despite earning hundreds of thousands of dollars a year, still struggled to find money each month to pay the bills. Why? Well maybe they watched the movie *Wall Street* one too many times, but at the end of the day, like many of us, they got caught up living a label. They bought a Porsche (and the repayments killed them), rented a decadent apartment, and lived L-A-R-G-E Puff Daddy style. It's the image of the mover and shaker.

Unfortunately, even though they're earning tons of cash, most of it is spent maintaining the lifestyle. When I went into the stock-broking field my old man had one piece of advice for me, 'Don't turn into a wanker'. Dad, I think I've upheld my end of the bargain.

It's not just people on lots of cash that get caught up in the label game – to a certain degree all of us are affected. Let's look through the marketing madness and see it for the propaganda it is. Businesses are in the biz of malting consumers spend. How do they turn an otherwise generic bottle of water into something fashionable? By marketing. How do they convince you that you need to shell out £150 for a T-shirt that costs less than £5 to make? By marketing. They're not selling the shirt; they're selling a lifestyle – all the things that the marketing people have embodied in a brand. I might own a Real Madrid football shirt, but when I put it on I don't feel like David Beckham, or play football like him, unfortunately.

Britain has without doubt one of the highest standards of living anywhere in the world. By virtue of the fact that you are a resident of Britain you are already on top of the heap by global standards.

A survey by a United Nations development program ranks Britain in the top countries in the world in relation to real income, life expectancy and educational standards. That means we're doing a whole lot better than most people.

Dub dub dub files

Spend time fantasising about what it would be like to be rich?

It's time for a reality check: You're already one of the wealthiest people on the planet. Check out www.globatrichlist.com and get some perspective. Simply type in your annual income, and check out your global standing, from richest to poorest. The site uses figures from the World Bank's development research group.

The table input data is designed for US and UK figures.

My tour of duty

On my radio program, we have a big focus on travelling – be it back-packing, holidaying or working around the globe. Not only is it a hell of a lot of fun to do, but it also gives you perspective. I recently returned from a trip to South-East Asia, which truly jolted my perceptions of this country.

On my tour of duty I saw families living on the sides of roads. I saw them huddled together on my nightly walks, trying to keep warm and dry as the wet season set in. I also witnessed the slave labour that occurs when multinational companies set up sweatshops to pump out garments so that they can put a million per cent mark-up on them and sell the dream to vain Western consumers.

Many people in South-East Asia put up with substandard housing, intermittent electricity, poor telecommunications, unhygienic drinking water and food that is prepared in filthy conditions.

Number of people in the world living on less than £1.00 a day?
5 billion

Through it all the lasting impression that I received was that most people in South-East Asia seemed genuinely happy. Place the average Westerner in their shoes and it would be a catastrophe – or on second thoughts, it's probably already a hit reality TV show by now.

Some of the coolest people I know couldn't care less about keeping up with the Jones's, they live their own life and focus on achieving the things that mean something to them, not what anyone else has dictated. My view? I don't give a shit what clothes you wear, what brand of cola you drink, where you live, what you drive, so long as you're happy.

Talking 'bout my generation

The challenges we face building wealth in the new millennium

There have been a heap of studies lately that have highlighted the fact that the post-Baby Boomer generations are struggling with issues such as the soaring cost of home ownership, tertiary education, job insecurities and changes to the welfare system.

The deal is that we are seeing first-hand the effects of a generational shift. Baby Boomers are placing a massive burden on our

Baby Boomers	Generation Xers
Had access in real terms to more affordable housing	Have seen housing prices rise to such an extent that housing affordability is at a 13-year low
Were part of a much more resilient labour force	Have come to accept job insecurity as downsizing, rightsizing and casual employment become more popular
Were offered free university education	Have to pay for university through tuition fees and student loans

Source: Generation Xcluded: AMP.NATSEM Income & Wealth Report Issue 6. November 2003.

infrastructure as they all hurtle at breakneck speed towards retirement, the bungalow in Torquay and lawn bowls.

My parents are fond of saying, 'things ain't what they used to be', and for once they're dead right. Let's have a look at how some things have changed.

Housing

Baby Boomers have had access to cheaper housing (in real terms). You'd have to be living under a rock somewhere if you hadn't worked out that housing prices in the UK, US and Australia have reached insane levels.

Housing is one of the central issues that affect younger generations. It's becoming increasingly difficult for first home buyers to gain a foothold in the property market and, as the dream of home ownership slips further out of reach, younger generations are missing the opportunity to get in the game. Because of this I have included a detailed chapter on the housing market, including an analysis on what drives housing prices, that finishes with an action plan to get you into your very own McMansion.

One of the key points about getting ahead is that you will eventually need to start making money passively. What do I mean by that? Making money without having to work for it.

Home ownership is a perfect example. You purchase a home, start paying off your mortgage, and in ten, twenty, or thirty years your house (asset) should be worth a lot more than you originally paid for it.

Careers

Job security, or better yet job insecurity, has been highlighted as a major difference between the two generations. Remember when you quit school at sixteen, got a job, kept away from the boss's wife and ended up as a senior executive picking up your gold watch as you shook hands with the chairman of the company after forty years of loyal service? Neither do I, but apparently it happened once. A few things have happened since then.

First, younger generations have experienced the technological explosion that has made redundant much of the menial labour that was once the backbone of the workforce. At the same time there's been a steady increase in the use of casual labour, which has made establishing a career path more difficult for many younger workers.

Education

As a result of an uncertain labour market demand for education has skyrocketed and Generation X has become the most qualified generation in history. Almost 60 per cent of Generation Xers have tertiary qualifications. Years ago if you had been to university you were on the fast track to management. These days we hear about people with multiple degrees, even some with PhDs, who are still asking the crucial question: 'Do you want fries with that?'

Baby Boomers were offered free university education. Not so for the young people of today. The dreaded student loans has meant that university is certainly not free anymore – British students have racked up collective university debt of £14.6 billion, which will have to be repaid throughout their working lives.

Because of our tertiary education many of us have a crippling debt that takes a big chunk out of our pay packets every week. Sometimes we are forced to take a first job doing something that's completely different to what we've studied just to get 'some experience', not to mention the humbling experience of looking at housing prices and calculating that on our income we might just be able to afford a beach hut in Aberystwyth.

These days turned out nothing like I had planned
POWDERFINGER

The fabric of society is changing. Don't get me wrong – I'm not getting all Kurt Cobain depressed, I'm just highlighting the fact that we're living in different times to those of other generations, and therefore getting control of your money is even more essential to treading our own path.

Don't just passively read this book, take the time to think about how the different topics relate directly to you. If you do, you'll be better equipped for the journey.

The future is going to be expensive!

Prices keep going up. Economists with polyester ties and dandruff on their shoulders tell us it's a phenomenon called inflation. Just like the influx of reality television, inflation is here to stay, pushing up the price of most things as time goes by. What can we do about it?

My old man is always harassing me about how much a big night costs me.

I wake up, my head's pounding, I've got the dry throat, I'm trying to work out how I got home, and all I want is a gallon of water. I stumble out of my room and my parents are sitting down having, well, dinner, and are looking at me with the shame of having an alcoholic son.

Then Dad starts up: 'How much did last night's drunken episode cost you?'

I mumble 'eighty quid' – truthfully, without thinking, because I'm not at my best when I've just woken up. Usually I can see a set-up before I walk into it.

'Eighty pounds!' Dad screams incredulously. 'That's ludicrous, highway robbery boy! When I was your age ... ' And it's like – here we go. Church is in session, the Reverend is about to start another sermon.

The truth is when my old man was my age (some thirty years ago) a cleansing glass of ale set him back the grand total of 20 pence. Can you imagine that? The mind boggles: As in, I'm going out, going to have a huge night so I better dig into the savings. I'll take out ... three pounds! That'll buy me ten beers and I'll still have enough for the jukebox and for the taxi home.

I know what you're thinking, what a great time to be alive! Twenty cents for a beer! But hey, step back bucko, my old man was probably only earning eighty quid a week – and that was a full-time wage.

What I'm getting at here is inflation. Prices rising. Each year prices of everything from a beer, a car, food ... everything rises. According to the Office for National Statistics, the annual average since 1987 has been about 4 per cent.

This isn't so bad cos just like when my old man was hitting the club scene ... I wonder if they had clubs back then? Actually, on second thoughts, probably not ... Anyway he was only earning £80. So roughly speaking the price of a beer was relative to what the price of a beer is now. We just earn more. Each year as prices go up, economists tell us that our wages should (hopefully) increase by roughly the same amount. If they don't then we lose purchasing power because as prices rise our income will buy us a little bit less each year.

Like most things in finance, people tend to use confusing and intellectual terms for what are essentially simple concepts. Here's a classic example of what inflation is: remember being in primary school when the school bell rang at 3.30 pm, and you and your mates jumped on your bikes and rushed down to the sweetshop to get 20 pence worth of mixed lollies? While age has no doubt matured your palate, try finding a use for twenty pence now!

Going up and going down

We've established that inflation erodes our purchasing power over time – so the value of a pound today (using the historical average of 4 per cent inflation a year) is only 96 pence in a year's time.

I can already hear you saying, big deal, 4 per cent here, 4 per cent there, it's all sand through the hourglass.

When looked at with a measly dollar, or with our beer analogy, things still look pretty calm. It's when we apply the principle to larger ticket items that we see inflation can get a little scary. Here's how that 4 per cent kicks in over just one year.

The impact of inflation

	2004	2005
Stereo	£250	£260
Car	£12 500	£13 000
House	£200 000	£208 000
Guy Sebastian — Angels Brought Me Here	£14.975	£0.05

An important thing to point out is that there is no 'value added' in these prices. Inflation is simply an increase in price for what is essentially the same product. The examples that I have illustrated above basically mean that you will have to find more money as each year rolls on for essentially the same product.

That being said, certain items, like DVD players, computers, or any offering from a Pop Idol 'artist', may actually drop in value due to technology or manufacturing breakthroughs. At the same time other goods and services can rise in price faster than inflation. Good examples of this are growth investments – shares and property.

Yikes! Sounds like the future is going to be expensive!

Here's the deal. Inflation is a wild beast that is constantly eroding the value of the folding stuff in your back pocket. Each year that cash can purchase a little less than it did previously – while at the same time we want to be increasing our standard of living. Hmm, there's a conundrum that even Who *Wants To Be a Millionaire*'s Chris Tarrant would have trouble solving.

Enter investing.

To guard against inflation, people invest their money. Historically, certain types of investment, which we'll be talking about in depth later, will provide returns higher than the historical average of inflation, which is a process known in grammar schools as 'outpacing inflation' or, as I like to put it, staying ahead of the game.

But which assets should I invest in to keep playing ahead? Have I totally missed the boat?

Ahem ... yes. Take it easy tiger. This won't be on the test. Let's look at the historical returns of each of the major asset classes (an asset class is a term investors use that groups broad categories of different types of investments, like shares, property, fixed interest and cash, to compare general returns). They reveal two sets of figures: the annual returns for different types of assets and the all-important historical inflation adjusted annual returns for the asset classes, which is derived by subtracting the historical rate of inflation of 4 per cent from the annual returns.

One thing about using historical examples – they're just that, historical. They are used as a guide to the future based on what we know about the past. But one thing we can count on is that things *can* and *will* change in the future.

Annual returns by asset class over twenty years to mid-2005

Residential property	5.50%
Shares	10.60%
Fixed interest	9.90%
Cash	7.80%

Inflation-adjusted annual returns by assets class over twenty years to mid-2005

Residential property	1.80%
Shares	6.90%
Fixed interest	6.20%
Cash	4.10%

Goals

Money is simply pieces of paper (well plastic these days). It has no real value until you apply it to the things that are important to you – the achievement of the short, medium, and long-term goals that we've set for ourselves. Money has been and always will be a means to an end. What makes it sexy is using it effectively so we can achieve the things that mean the most to us.

I've always been interested in money – how to make it, how to invest it, and how to spend it. I'm what you call a money nut. That's my thing.

Through experience I've also learnt that most people would rather have a frank and open discussion with their parents as to why they're still single than to sit down and tackle personal finance, and I couldn't agree more.

For far too long personal finance has been the domain of the 'home on a Saturday night crowd' and I'm here to say that we shouldn't let them have all the fun. Investing is sexy goddamnit!

You picked up this book because at some level you recognise that learning about, and getting control of, your finances is worthwhile. What I'm here to tell you is that it's absolutely essential. While we may all believe that someday we're going to win *Big Brother*, the lottery, or be offered millions of pounds for our artistic endeavours, the likelihood of any of these happening is close to zip. What we are left with is reality.

The best thing about being young is that we have something more valuable than Richard Branson's piggy bank ... the opportunity right now to plan the next ten, twenty, thirty, (yikes!) fifty years of our lives.

What the Barefoot Investor is about is living the life you want, and helping you to use all your resources to get there – and that's the sexy part of being Barefoot. What's sexier than living a life of choice?

We all have goals that we want to achieve. Maybe it's to buy a house in the burbs and pump out some kids, maybe it's breaking free from the confines of the rat race. Janet Jackson and Luther Vandross were right, the best things in life are free – but in a cruel twist of irony having the cash in your back pocket allows you to spend the bulk of your time doing them. Going barefoot is about achieving the things that are important to you – my job is to provide you with a simple, down to earth plan to get you to that point (wherever that may be), as quickly and as efficiently as possible. When you have your finances in order you call the shots.

That's where this book differs from others. Going barefoot isn't about denying yourself the things that are important to you – it's the complete opposite. It's about recognising that you only live once and by getting smart about the money you earn now, you'll be able to live exactly the way you choose as the years roll by.

The fundamental principle behind the Barefoot Investor is that everything we do with our money from earning it, investing it and spending it should be centred on your goals. The only reason to invest (or earn for that matter) is to achieve the things that are most important to us.

Personally I want to make my own path, I don't want to be dictated to by my parents, partner, neighbour or friends – and with cash in my pocket I can. True independence is what we're ultimately chasing and it is the only reason we bother getting our money in order. It's certainly a sexy alternative to being the lap-dog of your parents, grandparents, significant other or bank.

What does money mean to me? It means choice. There's been a few times in my life that I've picked up my bat and ball and gone on home. I once endured a boss who was a complete jerk; I've had housemates who drove me crazy. In each situation having money allowed me the freedom of choice.

Kicking goals

While I don't want to sound like the motivational gurus – sometimes those Giants Within they bang on about are best left sleeping – some of what they say makes sense. I believe that we shape our destinies through our choices, and that each of us has the ability to achieve things far beyond our wildest dreams.

Research has revealed that only one out of a hundred people have any definite plan about where they want to see their lives in the future. Most people tend to have goals that are fuzzy, as in 'I'd like to do some travelling', or 'maybe it'd be cool to get a better job'.

It's also true that most people spend more time planning a holiday than they do setting out in concrete the things they'd like to do, see, experience and achieve. It's been said that if you don't have a plan for the way you live your life, you'll become part of someone else's plan. Having been out in the cold harsh world of gainful employment for a few years now, I see that this is undeniably true.

Before you get down to the nitty gritty of getting your finances in order you need to understand exactly why you're doing it in the first place.

Getting your finances in check is the purpose of many personal finance books. Far too often I've found that people in the financial education business seem to focus on the '*how*' instead of the '*why*' – as in 'why the hell am I bothering?'

My argument has always been that if you plan your goals and get motivated and inspired by them, the fundamentals of learning about your finances and taking control of them is easy – not to mention a hell of a lot of fun for those on the Barefoot path.

First shots

I like thinking big. If you're going to be thinking anything, you might as well think big
DONALD TRUMP

The deal is this: nothing's going to change until you make a commitment. Unless you set a goal worth striving for you're not going to have the necessary motivation to go the extra mile. Where do you see yourself in five years time?

Let's start by focusing on your lifestyle-based goals. These are tangible goals that will decide the way you live in the future. Don't for a minute think I'm leading you down the path of greed and materialism. The premise behind the Barefoot Investor is not focused on being greedy. By definition its about kicking off your shoes and making your own path in life, and that's exactly what we're going to focus on – the things that mean the most to you. After we've established these goals, we can look at the tools and strategies outlined in this book as a way to get you there quickly.

There are things that we're all naturally passionate about. For some it may be travelling, for others it may be contributing to a charity or community service. You may have a flair for artistic expression. Whatever. The key questions are: Where are you going? How are you going to get there?

I understand that for many people pondering what they're going to eat for lunch that day is exerting too much forward thinking, and I also know that people often get uncomfortable when they have to start thinking about their future.

As a fickle twentysomething I can personally attest to the fact that my goals change on a daily basis. I will also tell you that I certainly don't have a personal mission statement or any of the other self-help crap that people espouse. But early on I sat down and decided where my life was heading and came up with the following:

- I wanted to be self-sufficient, to have true financial independence so that I was free to live the life I wanted without the emotional guilt trip that financial dependence breeds.
- I wanted to travel. I needed to see Down Under. I needed to see what was beyond our shores and the only way for me to get perspective on the world outside my little patch was to travel and experience different cultures.

- I decided that the status symbols that society values so highly weren't that important to me, and I made a conscious decision not to buy into the marketing hype.
- I also decided that after years of share-house living I wanted to get my own pad, where I could come and go as I pleased and I didn't have to answer to anyone. After that I set a goal of owning my own home.
- Another thing that is important to me is winding down work sooner rather than later. While I love my job, I decided early on that as I got older I wanted to choose whether I wanted to work. If I am passionate about the work that I'm doing I can keep going full steam ahead for the enjoyment, but it won't be for the money. If I decide there is something more beneficial I can be doing with my time, then I can choose to do that.

These are my personal goals. I've included them to give you an idea about the sorts of things you may want to start thinking about. I'm certainly not advocating my goals as the correct path.

These goals, or ideals if you like, have given me the necessary motivation and inspiration to get my finances in order and to experience true independence.

You'll notice that I haven't gone into specifics. That will certainly come as you start thinking through your goals, but by thinking about what is important to you, and the type of life you want to live, you can take the first steps of working towards them.

You only get one shot, do not miss your chance to blow, this opportunity comes once in a lifetime yo
EMINEM

Long-term goals

Too many young people (including myself) have absolutely no idea how they want to fill up, say the next fifty or sixty years, and even thinking about it can be a pretty daunting task. But right now I'd like to get you to start thinking about how having money would enable you to experience the things that are important to you. It's important not to censor yourself in this process, although its equally important not to get too bogged down in the specifics – like I want a house on Miami's South Beach or Sydney Harbour with antique furniture, a swimming pool, a hot tub ... I think you get the point.

For your longer-term goals, focus on the things you're passionate about, and what you would like to do in your life: the experiences, the sights, where you may want to live, whether you'd like to own your own home, the charities or community organisations that you'd like to contribute to, maybe a goal of winding down work sooner rather than later.

Short-term goals

I've included a section here for you to write down some short-term and long-term goals. It's important to think about the ways in which having money would help your everyday life. Maybe paying off Mr Visa, treating yourself to a Sunday lunchtime session with your friends, having some emergency money set aside so you don't have to live from week to week. Maybe it's just experiencing true financial independence so that you no longer have to look to others for financial support.

In the next exercise, take five minutes to write down as many things that spring to mind.

Goal planning

Short-term goals

....

....

....

....

....

Long-term goals

....
....
....
....
....

How'd you go? By now hopefully your mind is starting to focus on how you can use your money to do the things that mean the most to you, and that's the start of all successful wealth creation.

As I say time and time again, if you focus on getting your finances in order simply because it's the right thing to do, it's never going to be a change that lasts indefinitely.

The next time you do some window-shopping, or the next time you go on a bender with your mates, you'll throw personal finance out the window – and who wouldn't?

The same goes with focusing on being rich – focusing on having money for money's salve is a lame way to live. Having large amounts of money should certainly not be your end goal. Money is a means to an end. Instead, focusing on what you can use your money to achieve is a powerful motivator and one that facilitates you in becoming active with your wealth creation. This will allow you to speed up the process of attaining your goals.

The next step is to take your most important short, medium and long-term goals and write them on a separate piece of paper. Look at the goals you've set yourself and do two things:

1. Put a price tag on the most important goals you've set.

2. Assign a realistic date you want to achieve them by.

It may be a month, six months, a year, ten years or more. It's important not just to have huge twenty-year life goals, but also short-term goals, like paying off your credit card or purchasing a new item of clothing.

Now as you look over your list there are going to be some goals that will take you longer to achieve than others, and that's fine. By highlighting how you want to use money, it allows you to attain your goals a hell of a lot quicker than by idly sitting back (hung over) each New Year's Day and making a wish list – then forgetting about it the next day.

Putting a price tag on your goals allows your brain to see a set figure; assigning a realistic date for its attainment allows you to look forward in anticipation. Most psychologists agree that humans are more apt to move when the facts are laid bare.

Now it's time to spice things up a little ...

Starting with your most important short-term goal we combine the time frame you've set for yourself and then divide that by the price tag you've assigned to it. This enables you to chunk down your goals into bite-sized tasks.

A typical example for a short-term goal might be:

Goal: Pay off my credit cards within 12 months.

Price tag: Well I have £3000 racked up, so durr, it's three big ones.

Breakdown: Twelve months divided by £3000 is £250 a month, which is roughly £60 a week.

Follow through this process with all the most important goals you've chosen. These goals will become the basis of your Barefoot Plan.

Now that you're set ...

If you've followed the drill, you should now have in front of you a list of the things that you'd like to achieve before you find yourself in sandals and socks. If so, take five, go pour yourself a drink and congratulate yourself for being one of the few people in this world who consciously plan their future.

You may be a little overwhelmed by the fact that you're going to have to earn a ton of money to achieve all of this, but don't stress – if you've been realistic, I can help you get there a lot quicker than you ever imagined.

The rest of the steps are designed specifically to introduce you to the tools, strategies and products that will enable you to achieve the goals you've set for yourself, and to give you practical advice on how to sort out your finances immediately.

Look Out for Number One

BAREFOOT STEP 2

Now you have your goals some way to being sorted, it's time to roll your sleeves up and get a little dirty. In this step we're going to:

- Introduce you to the principle of Barefoot Bondage, which will give you the discipline to achieve your goals and tread your own path.
- Get you spending more of your cash on the things you really want.

- Show you how you can get more mojo in your life.
- Help you get the best deal on your everyday bank account.
- Look at bank accounts that pay high interest and have no bank fees.
- Look at a nifty strategy that'll mean you never have to go scrounging in the cushions of the couch to pay your monthly bills again.

This step lays the foundations for hassle-free money management forever!

Control your cash

Truth or dare. *OK truth*!

I've never ever stuck to a budget ... ever!

I have more important things to do than spending an afternoon budgeting out every last cent of my pay cheque, and I certainly don't waste my time fretting over every little purchase that I make. The thought of adhering to the typically anal retentive budget that I've seen espoused elsewhere is something I've never had the discipline (or patience) to stick to.

I promised the Barefoot Plan wouldn't require much willpower and I meant it. The only way to control your spending is to get excited about spending more of it on things you really want.

Nifty little budgets where you allocate your wage down to the last few cents aren't going to achieve the change in mindset that's required. We need to take a radically different approach to spending cash – and in the process direct your spending habits towards what you want most.

Barefoot Bondage
—some light discipline so you can tread your own path

It's now time to introduce you to a strategy known as 'Barefoot Bondage'. The hardest thing about getting your finances sorted is summoning the discipline to stay on track, day in day out, without giving in to temptation ... ever.

Before I got into a lil' Barefoot Bondage, my cash would go quicker than Elton John. Like most people, at the end of each financial year I receive a P60 certificate that outlines my earnings over the previous twelve months. Up until I sorted myself out a few years ago, most years the figure almost gave me heart palpitations as I looked at the total, and asked myself the eternal question ... Where did it all go?

If you're like most people, the day you get paid you feel rich so you treat yourself a little. Maybe you buy a magazine, grab a coffee or lunch with your mates. Then, over the course of a couple of days, you find yourself making more frequent trips to the ATM to withdraw cash. Fifty pounds here, twenty pounds there, and suddenly by about midweek, you start to wonder where all your money has gone.

Instead of beating myself up, I looked at where I wanted my money to go and decided to start making some changes that would allow me to get there quicker, without feeling like I was depriving myself. Enter Barefoot Bondage.

When I speak about directing all your money towards the things that mean the most to you, most people agree that in theory it's a smart way to operate, with the emphasis being on the 'in theory'.

In theory budgets are a fantastic idea, and we all know that we'd be better off if we could direct our cash to the things we really want. Unfortunately life isn't theoretical – life is walking to work and buying a Red Bull to wake yourself up before you face the boss, it's about going out for dinner with your friends to celebrate a special occasion, it's about parking fines.

I certainly can't claim credit for the methods that I am about to introduce you to (most of them have been around in some form for many years), although I can claim that I have tried everything under the sun to curtail my spending habits and I'm delivering the very best of it to you.

No whips, chains or chaps required

The tools for the Barefoot Bondage strategy are separate (high-earning) bank accounts, an envelope and knowledge of your spending habits.

The restraint comes from setting up different bank accounts for different purposes, and getting your payroll officer to transfer the funds in directly each pay day.

Having your pay dumped into the one account is a recipe for disaster. Seeing a big balance on pay day for most of us (me included) is like waving a red rag at a bull. By directing small amounts of your money into different accounts, and making sure it's not instantly accessible every time you have the urge to splurge, the combined force of a high rate of interest and regular deposits mean you'll achieve your goals in no time.

One of the fundamental principles of this book is to pay yourself first. People tend to spend a lot of time paying Mr Visa, Mr Orange, Ms Ikea and Mr Sky before they bother to pay themselves!

Too many of us look at investing from completely the wrong angle. Investing isn't a blood sport, it's not one big giant fruit machine, and it's certainly not something you wait until you've saved up fifty grand to do – it's the little amounts socked away regularly that turn people into millionaires. Ten per cent of your income is the goal – and saving 15 per cent will put you well on your way to building serious cash.

The most important thing to do is contribute something, anything, just start doing it. I guarantee within a couple of weeks your mind will get in the groove and as your balance goes up, you'll get up to 10 per cent in no time.

Investing for the future – whether it be for a year or a lifetime, is something that's as simple as paying your phone bill each month. You are the most important person in your world. It's time to start treating yourself that way.

Figuring out where your money goes

The only way to work out how to do this is by doing some research. There's a lot to be gained by taking a good hard look every now and again at where your money is going and, more importantly, figuring out where you want it to go.

So I have included a worksheet for you to fill in what your day-to-day expenses are. Now don't get me wrong, the exercise I'm getting you to do certainly isn't the basis of a budget, so don't feel guilty about your spending discretions – it's merely a quick way to work out where your cash has been going.

Try to fill this out as honestly and factually as possible. Go to the bank and request a statement of your savings account for the last couple of months (you can usually obtain this online) so you can get an accurate picture of where you spend your money.

Spend a few minutes entering in the amounts into the graph, and then multiply each weekly subtotal by 52. By answering as truthfully as possible you'll get the cold hard facts on where your money is going.

Day-to-day expenses

	£ PER WEEK	MULTIPLY BY 52	£
HOUSING			
Rent/Mortgage repayments	....	....	....
House Insurance	....	....	....
Electricity	....	....	....
Gas	....	....	....
Telephone (fixed and mobile)	....	....	....
Satellite TV	....	....	....
Video rental	....	....	....
Internet	....	....	....
Other	....	....	....
FOOD			
Groceries	....	....	....
Coffee's, cokes, snacks	....	....	....
Purchased lunches	....	....	....
Takeaways	....	....	....
Restaurants	....	....	....
Other	....	....	....
TRANSPORT			
Car repayments	....	....	....
Petrol	....	....	....
Car Insurance	....	....	....

Registration ....
Congestion charges ....
Car maintenance ....
Public transport ....
Parking ....
Taxis ....
Other ....

REPAYMENTS

Credit cards ....
Personal loans ....
Student loans ....
Store cards ....
Other ....

HEALTHCARE

Health insurance ....
Prescriptions ....
Dental ....
Doctor's visits ....
(massage, chiropractor included)
Hairdresser ....
Beauty ....
Gym memberships ....
Sporting equipment/fees ....
Cosmetics & toiletries ....
Other ....

EVERY TIME THE NEED ARISES ...

Partying ....
Kebabs at 3 am ....
Concerts ....
CD's ....

Dry cleaning	....	....	....
Magazines, newspapers, books	....	....	....
Clothes	....	....	....
Gifts	....	....	....
Holidays	....	....	....
Household furnishings	....	....	....
School fees, and supplies	....	....	....
Job related expenses (non reimbursed)	....	....	....
Other	....	....	....

* Some of these items aren't going to fit into a neat 'weekly' spending pattern. Get out a calculator and try and average them down to a weekly cost to give yourself a good understanding of where your cash goes.

As you look down your list if you're like most people there'll be at least a couple of surprises there that until now you hadn't really paid much attention to.

From little things big things grow
PAUL KELLY AND KEV CARMODY

Let's say you buy a latte every morning on the way to work. 'No big deal,' you say, 'it's only £1.50. I'm earning good money, I can afford it'. Well yeah, you can, but it's not really a question of that.

If you buy a one-fifty coffee every morning that's going to set you back £7.50 a week or nearly £390 a year. If you forgo your morning hit of caffeine and instead make a regular cup of Joe when you get to work – or alternatively get one of those groovy travel coffee mugs and make one from home, would your life be diminished in any way?

Now let's look at the yearly expense – £390, what could you do with that £390 that would make a difference to you? Well, you could probably have a fairly good week away with friends; you could purchase a stereo, pay your car tax or insurance, buy some new clothes, the list is endless. Think back to the goals that you've been thinking about. Three hundred and ninety pounds would go a long way to putting a dent in at least one of them.

Having said that, if a morning caffeine hit is your idea of heaven and you couldn't think of getting up in the morning without it – and you've considered the alternatives that you'll be forgoing – and you're still thinking that your morning hit is worth it, by all means enjoy the coffee, and give yourself a pat on the back – at least you've thought it through and made a decision that's rational.

Putting the plan into action

This strategy requires you to direct your pay into three different bank accounts (for a guide to choosing the right ones check out Robbing Banks on page 45):

- **An everyday banking account**
- **High-yielding account No 1 for the goals you wrote down in the first step**
- **High-yielding account No 2, known as the Mojo account**

Getting your payroll officer to pay directly into your different accounts is by far the best way to do it. This way you never see the money pass through your hot little hands.

In all the different organisations I've worked at, I'm yet to have to resort to any underhand methods to get the payroll person to split my pay, although if need be you can certainly get a direct debit out of your nominated bank account each pay day and shoot it off to different accounts.

The bank accounts I recommend for this budgeting philosophy are the high-yielding interest-based savings accounts that are linked to your normal everyday bank accounts. The kicker is that most of these accounts don't charge bank fees (we'll tackle bank fees later). They're predominantly net-based so start using the web for things other than surfing for porn and checking your horoscope. For details of these check out robbing banks on page 45.

What goes where?

Everyday banking account

Due to the abysmal interest rate that most conventional bank accounts pay, you should only keep your day-to-day expenses here. Any surplus cash should be transferred to a higher yielding alternative. The first thing you need to do is sit down and take a realistic look at how much moolah is needed to maintain your lifestyle.

→ **First: gather the info**

Let's look at your wage. How much cash are you bringing home?

Next, take a look at your weekly and monthly spending habits as outlined on pages 38–39. Look at where your money is going, with the emphasis on trimming the fat.

No need to join a monastery

Sometimes people get a little carried away when they perform budgets and allocate themselves a ridiculously small amount of money for daily expenses. Take it from me, you may last a few weeks getting by being a complete tightarse, but the real issue here is to start being responsible about the money that you earn and spend, not to commit yourself to a monastery and start self-flagellating.

Really, it's up to you what you decide to do with your money, but you've got to have a good look at where you spend it, where you can cut back and, importantly, where you can direct it.

It's also important to make sure that your daily expenses cover the left field experiences that always seem to happen to you as soon as you decide to get your spending under control – like going out on a date, going to the movies, or out for a drink after work. Give yourself a little padding and you'll be more apt to stick to the plan and won't feel as though you're denying yourself.

By completing this you should have a fixed amount that you can comfortably get by on a day-to-day basis for each pay period.

→ Second: my name is Stan, and I have a plan

Now you have your daily money sorted, I'd encourage you to use the envelope system for paying your bills. It works like this: each week you take out a certain amount of cash (that covers your recurring bills) and put it into an envelope, which is ominously called the bill file.

By being disciplined to place the money in the envelope each week you get paid, and sticking to it, you'll be able to effectively allocate, and gain control of your money. Knowing you have money set aside to meet your commitments is a great feeling.

One of my best examples was the £20 I put away for utilities (gas/electricity etc.), the regular household bills. I made sure that I put it in the envelope every week, regardless of whether I had any bills due that month. Every time a bill came in, I always had the cash to meet it, and never had to scrounge around or go without anything else to pay it. At the end of the year, I had around £200 left over in that envelope. So like any fine upstanding young man I invested it ... Christ no! I went out and blew the lot! The cool thing was it was like a bonus that I'd been paid. There is no way I would have had that cash if I hadn't followed this system.

So grab an envelope and using the information you wrote down on the budget on pages 38–39, work out how much you'll need to cough up each month in bills and put that amount of cash into the envelope each pay period.

Savings account no 1

The second account is set up specifically to save for our goals. It's time to get serious about our goal setting that we did in the first chapter. You'll remember that we outlined our goals, assigned a realistic date for their attainment and then put a price tag on them. It's now time to allocate a set amount of money towards them, and get your payroll officer to direct the cash each time you are paid.

Savings account no 2: The Mojo account

My mojo's working overtime, baby!
AUSTIN POWERS

Mojo, the force that gives us that little bit of magic to deal with life's sticky situations, can work for us in cash terms too. Here's how ...

After you've been realistic about your weekly necessities, the next step is to set up your Mojo account. A Mojo account acts as your personal buffer zone – your mojo, so to speak, and its prime purpose is to give you confidence and peace of mind. Your Mojo account will over time become your passport to wealth ... but I'm getting ahead of myself. Best I explain how it works first.

The deal is that you allocate 10 per cent of your income to the Mojo account you've set up. Regardless of how often you get paid, deposit a regular amount each pay period. Let's say you earn £500 a week before taxes – £450 in your hand, so you deposit £45. I can already hear it now. Shave off 10 per cent!? Is this guy crazy? I can't afford that! Before you start to question my sanity I'm going to let you in on a little secret ... you won't miss it. Well maybe you will the first week or two, but after a while it's a scientific fact that your mind adjusts. If you get only one thing out of this entire book, let it be that you set up a Mojo account. It's the key.

Your Mojo account is not an account that is drawn upon readily. It

Mojo Money

Putting 10 per cent of your wages into your Mojo account is something I strongly encourage you to do. I also realise that everyone's different, and that 10 per cent may be unrealistic for some battling to get by.

Don't let that put you off getting it started. Start with 1 per cent (and gradually work your way up) of your pay if need be—just do it.

The principles behind the Mojo account have made people millionaires. I want you to be one of them.

simply keeps getting added to each pay period, and inches up little by little, bit-by-bit. You'll be surprised how quickly it starts adding up, because in essence you're adhering to all the correct rules of saving – making regular contributions, not redrawing it and throwing into the mix a great rate of interest.

Primarily the Mojo account comes in handy when things start rocking your karma. Housemates unbearable? Move out of the dungeon and into something a little more tranquil using the Mojo account to smooth the moving costs. Got a boss who's the reincarnation of Mr Burns? Do a Homer Simpson, take a walks from the job and live off your Mojo account for a while.

The Mojo account is set up to give you some choices. With cash in your back pocket, specifically set aside for when trouble brews, you can choose to cop it sweet or use your monetary power like a get-out-of-jailfree card on a Monopoly board.

I've had a Mojo account running for years, and the secret to the account isn't in the actual money that keeps piling up month in, month out. The true secret behind the Mojo account is simply knowing it's there. It's the ace up my sleeve.

Although I've often been tempted to cash in my chips and use the cash when certain situations became a little tough, I never have, and today I can afford a pretty big mojo moment should anything serious happen to me.

It won't take long before you start to build up considerable mojo money in your account. In Step 4 of the Barefoot Plan we turbo charge the money by investing it (with as little as £2 a day). Peace of mind baby, yeah!

Robbing banks
—choosing the accounts for Barefoot Bondage

Choosing an everyday bank account may not be high on your priority list, but how about you throw a video in and tape *How Clean is your House?*, and spend half an hour or so analysing your monetary movements. Then pick a banking alternative that suits you – it could end up saving you thousands of dollars over the years.

Next up it's time to look at where you're storing your cash and rob some banks. So get out your stockings and place them over your head, get a sawn-off shotgun and let's go rip-off some banks!

You have a bank account. If you're like me, it was probably your parents' bank, and there was a branch nearby. Now if you're like most people this is probably the first time you've really thought about the bank you use. In fact if you're like most people I know, the last time you found yourself standing in a bank queue you were wearing happy pants and grooving along to Vanilla Ice's 'Ice Ice Baby' on your Walkman.

Most people agree that bank accounts have become increasingly generic. They're basically a card linked to your savings account that pays a minuscule amount of interest and a hole in the wall that dispenses cash. The statement comes around every three months or so, and its usually far too painful to read so you either throw it out before opening it (after all you keep a running balance in your head), or if you're a real masochist you'll open it and see what sort of financial shape you're in.

According to a report by the Reserve Bank Australians spent $437 million in transaction fees arising from foreign ATM charges in the last year alone.

I rob banks because that's where the money is
WILLIE SUTTON

When you start deducting your money from the bank they will charge you. Maybe you've got some sort of a deal whereby you get five transactions a month free then you pay for the rest. Whatever. If you're like most people you could be running up £5 to £10 a month in bank charges. Now you're being charged for the privilege. If you've still got the bank statement that you were working from in the previous section, add up your fees!

The alternative, you ask? Get an account that suits the way you bank.

Bank fees—the enemy

British banks generally don't make charges for personal current accounts provided they stay in credit. But go overdrawn and you can get hit with some mega fees. The banks make it back because they don't pay much interest (as in fractions of 1 per cent) on the balance that sits in your account while you are in the process of spending it. Most of us put up with this. We need to pull our heads out of the sand and start looking at different ways of maximising what our hard earned cash earns.

ATM addict

The real kicker with ATMs is withdrawing money from another bank's machine. In the business the banks call these 'foreign trans- actions' and they charge like a wounded bull. There is absolutely no bigger waste of money than making foreign transactions, it's just another way the banks cream money off the top of consumers who are too lazy to get their banking sorted and ensure they are with a bank that has ATMs in places that are convenient and easily accessible.

What happens when a bank robber calls?

Armed with this information it's wheeling and dealing time. Call your bank to negotiate a better deal. Always remember that as a fee- paying customer you have the power. A typical conversation may go like this:

Bank: Welcome to XYZ Bank. How can I help you?

You: About bloody time! I've been stuck on hold for twenty-five minutes for Christ sakes! Is this one of those dodgy call centres located in India? Did you have to swim over there to connect my call?

Bank: Your comments are appreciated.

You: OK, here's the deal: I've gone through my last couple of bank statements and analysed the way I facilitate my banking.

The current account that I'm using doesn't suit my needs as I use the Internet and a debit card as my main sources of banking.

I'm not in your branches and yet I'm earning next to nothing on my current account balance.

Do you have another account that will actually pay me a decent rate of interest if I stay in credit?

Bank: Hmm. Let me see ...

You: How's the weather in Bombay?

Bank: Your comments are appreciated. Thank you for waiting. We have a number of packages that focus on customers who use the Internet and debit card as their main ways of banking. These would boost the interest you earn quite a bit.

You: Sounds good. Send me the information ASAP. I'll look over the fine print and decide if it's a goer.

What happens if your bank doesn't come to the party?

Lets say that you called your current bank but they were less than helpful. Screw them. You're the customer. Cut your allegiances and turn yourself into a 'rate tart' to find the best paying account.

Big Banks versus Smaller Banks

Bohemian banks

In the UK the big banks are all becoming more generic; they're financial behemoths that are trying to grab each other's market share. But let's not tar all of them with the same banking brush – there are exceptions.

Many of these alternatives offer better services than the big banks because they are smaller and more focused on delivering the goods to their customers, who ultimately pay their wages by directing their banking their way.

The downside to straying from the big banking boys is that many lack ATMs in convenient places. Sure, you may be getting your account-keeping fees for a song, but it will quickly get eaten up if you have to use other banks' ATMs every second of the day, and be slugged an outlandish fee (around £1.50 a pop) each time you withdraw.

It goes without saying that all institutions, be it the big banks, the little banks or building societies all have their advantages and drawbacks. The main thing to focus on is how you do your banking.

Monogamous banking

Although the banks are doing fantastically well for their shareholders, they don't necessarily do so well by you, the customer. Remember, no one institution can best service all your needs.

In order to find the right products for yourself you need to compare what's on offer from as many different parties as possible, and get impartial advice.

Choosing a high-yielding account for your savings, and mojo money

The accounts to use are online high-interest savings accounts, and the main advantages of them are:

- No charges whatsoever.
- They earn a high rate of interest while you save for your goals.
- They're designed with the saver in mind, and don't have debit cards attached to them, which makes it that little bit harder to put on your captain consumer hat and splurge your savings.

Forget trawling the web for Paris Hilton pics, for me the net is now all about where I do my electronic banking. Sad, or what? But these are high-yielding (interest-paying) savings accounts linked to your general bank account.

The great thing about these accounts is that in most cases there's no minimum balance, so you can start earning a great return on your money with just a pound. You can jump on, transfer money over from your linked everyday account, earn a great rate of interest and, when you need the cash all you do is transfer it back over to your linked bank account, and the next business day it's there ready to roll. They're pure unadulterated, net-driven, financial porn.

From my personal experience, these accounts usually have good customer service – most offer telephone and Internet banking. As this book goes to print some of the companies offering E accounts are ING Direct, Cahoot, Smile, and Standard Life Bank (although as they become more popular they're popping up all over the place. Check financial websites and the financial papers to see what's on offer).

Banking sorted

In light of the big four banks' billion pound profits, which are largely made up of money from our pockets, don't feel intimidated about calling your bank and demanding a better deal. You are the consumer, and you have the power.

In short, the choice is yours. There is no one good account, nor one good institution to bank with. If you analyse the way you do your banking, and try to find an account and an institution that best suits your needs, you may well be hundreds of pounds better off each year. The choice is yours.

Becoming conscious

If you've taken the time to do the exercises contained

in Step 2, you'll start to see how easy it is to get ahead financially and how we all tend to spend money on junk without ever really becoming aware of it.

I've seen the strategy of Barefoot Bondage allow people to take overseas holidays, buy great clothes, or make other big purchases they normally wouldn't have been able to afford.

It sounds simple and it is. It's also one of the time-honoured ways to make you rich. So why don't more people do it?

Repo Your Repayments

BAREFOOT STEP 3

The third step in the Barefoot Plan involves:

- Breaking the rat race mentality.
- Taking control of outrageous mobile bills.
- Looking at death by plastic, rewards points, and the best way to manage your credit card.
- The truth behind those 'interest free' store offers.
- Showing you how to check your credit history and make sure there's no nasty surprises lurking.

- Answering the eternal question. Should I pay off my student loan?

The step finishes with a comprehensive action plan to get you out of debt quickly.

More money more problems

My university days were the best of my life. I rigged my course load so that I had permanent four-day long weekends each semester. Studying was strictly confined to the fortnight before exams, which left my motley group of mates and I plenty of time to pursue the art of brewing (and drinking) copious amounts of homebrew, partying most nights and spending the best part of the day sleeping while the rest of the world did the responsible thing.

Fine dining wasn't really on the top of my agenda, about as fine as the dining got was going to a restaurant that offered the dubious 'all you can eat buffet'. My diet consisted mainly of kebabs (usually at three in the morning), two-minute noodles, pizza and beer.

Being poor students meant that money was always in short supply. When it came, usually in the form of a parental endowment, or a new student loan, it was quickly and efficiently spent. We were accustomed to having 'a fiver to last till next Wednesday'. Feats of lasting literally days on the gastric concoction of baked beans and home brew were worn as a badge of honour.

After we graduated and got full-time jobs it was time to celebrate (even though our salaries weren't anything special). After spending years living below the poverty line, we could finally all start being grown-ups. I remember being at our graduation party and talking about how much easier life would be now that there was finally a full-time wage in our lives.

Over the space of a couple of years most of my mates are in a worse position than they were when they were at university. One of the guys who was proud to be driving a Mini that had half a million miles on the clock is now driving a shiny black BMW. A girl I once lived with used to fashion our house with hand-me-down couches and stolen street signs. She is now shopping at Harrods, blowing six months of her salary on decking out her (rented) living room. Most are carrying credit card debts and paying off car loans or personal loans.

Through my years as a stockbroker and helping people with different levels of income I've noticed that, for most people, expenses rise to meet their income, and then some.

Some people get their first full-time job and celebrate by going out and rewarding themselves with all manner of expensive purchases, secure in the fact that they are now in the workforce and their ever-increasing salary will more than accommodate the repayments. The problem is that it can take them the next seven or eight years of their working lives to pay off the debts they incurred as a celebration of joining the workforce.

Because of this, it takes most people a lot longer to experience true financial independence. They spend the bulk of their pay cheques on debts, wondering how they'll ever get the opportunity to do the things that they really want to do.

Debt

Tyler Durden, Brad Pitt's character in *Fight Club*, was right. Many of us have become enslaved by our possessions. We buy stuff that we can't afford to, chase the lifestyle that society tells us means success, and spend most of our working lives struggling to pay it back.

In his recent bestseller *Growth Fetish*, Australian economist Clive Hamilton showed that wealth fails to make people happier. The exception is the poor, whose increased happiness when they get richer is entirely related to meeting basic needs like food on the table, adequate housing and clothing. For the rest of us, rampant consumerism is a dead end. Many people trapped in high-paying jobs to pay off their debts dream of a simpler, less stressful life.

Personal debt levels have soared in recent years, fed by our love of plastic. According to Datamonitor, the amounts outstanding on unsecured debt (that's credit cards and personal loans to you and me) rose 45 per cent between 2000 and 2004 and last year the average Brit owed £1302 on credit cards, £1892 on personal loans and £812 on overdrafts and car and store loans. We Brits are now finding ourselves in a situation where housing debt and personal debt is rising faster than disposable income, which is kind of like walking to McDonald's for the exercise – then eating five McHappy meals as a reward.

Fulfilment can't be purchased on a gold card

A word of warning – I am completely prejudiced when it comes to personal debt such as credit cards, personal loans, car loans and interest free loans. Personal debt is clueless and, dear reader, you can quote me on that.

Where's your head at?
BASEMENT JAXX

Why am I so against personal debt? Because it cheats us out of achieving the goals that we've set for ourselves. The goal of the Barefoot Investor is to get you to a point where you experience true financial independence, which will then enable you to make the choices to do the things that mean something to you.

The problem is compounded when you take a look at the interest rate that lenders are charging you on this type of debt. Usually it's far above the rate that home owners are paying off their mortgage. In effect you are being charged with a loser tax because you haven't worked out a way to budget (or go without) for things that fall in value.

The bottom line is that at some point in time you have to pay back the debt you've accumulated, and until you do you're essentially owned by whomever you owe money to. Think I'm over exaggerating?

Let's look at a typical situation that a lot of people are in. Say you're on a fairly standard wage of £20 000 a year. Let's also assume that you have a penchant for plastic and have racked up £3000 on your cards.

What are your options? What choices do you have about taking some time off work, falling ill for an extended period, or being made redundant? Or what about the option of simply taking some much needed rest and relaxation? Sweet FA.

With debt you've got to keep bringing home the bacon. Well you're not actually bringing home the bacon, you're not even putting the bacon towards paying off a house, you're merely slapping down some of your hard earned pieces of pig on stuff that you probably have expended and long forgotten about – and that stinks. Even if you hate your job you have little choice but to keep working. My goal is to get you to true financial independence, and to enable you to live life on your terms.

Good debt v bad debt

You'll often hear financial types speak of good debt and bad debt. Here's the lowdown. Debt in its simplest form is borrowing money to finance the purchase of things you need and/or want. How we use this debt is where the classifications come in. If we use debt to purchase things that increase in value such as a home, to fund an investment property or invest in shares, otherwise known as assets, this is classified as good debt.

Borrowing money for things that fall in value is known as bad debt. Most of this debt is classified as personal debt and includes borrowing money for expensive cars (some new cars can fall in value up to

30 per cent or more in the first year alone), to fund retail therapy by way of credit cards, or personal loans for things you can't afford like holidays.

History lesson

For this lesson we're going to need those purveyors of practicality, your mum and dad. I'd like you to ask them two very simple questions:

Question 1: The price of their first home and – if Alzheimer's hasn't kicked in – the size of their initial mortgage.

Qustion 2: The make and model of the first car they bought, and what it cost them.

Incidentally, when I did this exercise with my parents it unleashed a flurry of reminiscing that left me in a state of extreme numbness, the likes of which I haven't experienced since the guy from accounts cornered me at last year's office Christmas party. They recounted e-v-er-y detail of what life was like 'back then'. Agree. Quickly. Move on.

OK, now that we've established the answers to the two questions above, delve a little deeper:

- What would the price of the house your parents first bought be (roughly) now?
- Is the mortgage your parents took out for their first place roughly the same amount of money that today you'd spend partying for a couple of weeks in Ibiza?
- Ask your old man how much he'd get for his first car (if it was still going) today?
- Ask which investment gave them more fulfilment?
- When they look back on it, which purchase had the biggest effect on their quality of life?

I know, I know, giving your parents the ability to talk about the good old days, coupled with the double whammy of giving them an excuse for a lecture, isn't cutting the mustard, but sit back and ponder the answers to those questions.

Delving into debt

Instant gratification

We all know the excuses we make for ourselves, they are endless: I was feeling down. I thought I'd treat myself. It was a once in a lifetime opportunity. Twenty per cent off at River Island, h-e-l-l-o? I'll worry about how to pay for it later. I'm going to knuckle down – starting next week.

Everyone has an excuse when they buy things they can't afford. As many different excuses as there are, the result is nearly always the same – a credit hangover that lingers longer than the thirteenth cocktail you had at last year's Christmas party.

If you frequently buy stuff you can't afford, whacking it on fantastic plastic you're delaying the pain. If you can't afford to purchase it with cold hard cash, get your head out of the Ikea catalogue and think. Sure, modern society has provided us with a whole host of convenient services that allow us to spend money we don't have on stuff we don't really need, but at the end of the day, you're treading your own path. This 'convenience' comes at a price – the freedom to do the things you want, whenever you want.

You wouldn't credit it

Every generation learns their lessons at some stage; history repeats itself. Many older folk who lived through the (not so) great depression would be shocked to see the blasé attitude that people these days have towards credit.

I once dated a girl who, for legal reasons, we'll call Sarah. She's got a fantastic job as a marketing executive at a big firm, which nets her fifty big ones a year. This girl's got it sorted – great job, great accessories, funky flat in docklands. When the editors of *Cosmo* and *Cleo* define their target audience they're thinking of Sarah. Other people watch *Sex and the City* – this girl *lives* it.

From the outside looking in she's got it all going on, but after a few dates she levelled with me: 'I've got a £5000 credit card debt and it's killing me. The repayments are £100 a month, and it's really getting me down.' Understanding that I was a financial type, she wanted answers on how to get herself out of the hole she was in.

Now as many of my ex-girlfriends will attest, most of the time I like to play dumb, so the first thing I asked her was, 'What did you borrow the money for?' She looked a little perplexed. 'What do you mean?' she asked. 'You're five grand in debt, obviously you borrowed the money for something. So was it for a holiday? A car? Furniture?'

Her answer was the same as 90 per cent of the people I counsel who have racked up large amounts of personal debt – she had no idea. I find most people who have big debts haven't used their credit for anything tangible that has added to their lives. They've learned to live on debt, and it's a dangerous pastime. It's one of the major causes of wealth destruction. Getting into a cycle of living beyond your means (spending more money than you earn) means you're essentially a slave to your possessions, and unless you change you're never going to be able to experience true financial freedom.

I owe, I owe, so it's off to work I go

When I was at university I worked as an intern at one of the major banks. I used to sit next to a middle-aged lady who had a comical cartoon of the twelve dwarves stuck to the top of her computer screen, with the rather amusing play on words, 'I owe, I owe, so it's off to work I go'. This lady was always complaining to me that she never had any cash, while at the same time she was always buying junk off those lame infomercials. She had the hair wand, the abdominizer, the steak knives, and the twenty-one days to total transformation cassette workshop.

I owe, I owe, so it's off to work I go. What type of crack was she smoking? Why would anyone force themselves to work just so they could pay off crap they didn't really need in the first place?

Look, don't get me wrong here, I am not talking about purchasing stuff like everyday household goods and things you need like groceries or paying the gas bill. I'm talking about lattes, I'm talking about dinners out, partying, clothes. I'm talking about all the things you have a choice whether you save up and buy with your own money or whack it on a credit card and pay later. It's not pay later – it's bend me over later because the average charges of credit card companies, as we are about to see, are insane.

Green with envy

Keeping up with the Jones's. Everyone suffers from it from time to time. Human beings are programmed to want to achieve, to compete. It's a throwback to the hunter and gatherer days where the caveman with the biggest club won the cavegirl.

In my group of friends it was all about cars. Not fast and the furious mind you, but there was a fair amount of unspoken rivalry about the type of car you drove.

Now I'm a stockbroker, and that title alone conjures up images of a decadent lifestyle – but while all my mates drove around in late-model Audis, luxurious four-wheel drives, and top-of-the-range BMWs, I drove a 1987 Datsun, ominously named the 'Datsun of Death'.

I once met up with an old flame from my uni days who, reminiscing, said, 'Whatever happened to that old heap you drove around back then, the 'Datsun of Death' – did you have to pay to get that thing towed away in the end?'

I explained that I was still driving that same piece of crap. Bring on the awkward silence ... Nothing says 'hello ladies' like a fifteen-year-old family sedan, with a coat-hanger for an aerial and dents in every panel.

My friends were dubious about my job – was I actually a cleaner at the stockbroking firm? After all, if I was making good money, why didn't I have a nice car?

I explained to them that I was making the choice between driving a nice car and spending my money on other things. Don't get me wrong, I'd love to have a nice new shiny car to drive around in. I've often been caught glancing just a little too long when I get to the cars' classified section of the paper – but it's just not for me.

The reason wasn't due to the actual cost of buying a car, but because my priorities were different to theirs. I didn't see the need to spend £20 000 on a car that I spent less than ten hours a week in (and in three years' time have it worth about £7000). I'd rather put up with driving the Datsun of Death and put that money towards a house. At least, I reasoned, if I put my money in a house or shares it would be worth progressively more – not less – as time went on. Besides, I spend much more time in a house than in my car.

Unfortunately for a lot of my friends, the desire to have a shiny car has meant that many of them are paying off a loan for a car that is rapidly decreasing in value. Most of them are now at the age where they want to start looking to buy a home, and are finding that they have to start all over again.

Sadly the Datsun of Death eventually lived up to its name and died on the way back to the country on a Friday night not so long ago. Much like a nag that's run its last meet, the Datsun of Death will spend her retirement in a paddock watching life go by.

In the end we all compete against each other to some degree. By looking at the things that are most important to you, and then setting out an action plan to achieve them, the only person you'll have to compete with is yourself.

Mobile phones

I love my mobile phone. I couldn't imagine life

without it. That doesn't mean I put up with outrageous monthly bills and neither should you – here's how to get on top of it.

When I was at school, no-one had a mobile phone. These days I see primary school children chatting away on their Nokias. Mobile phones have become more popular than a Zimmer frame at a retirement home – there are now more mobile phone owners than fixed line subscribers. There are now 50 million mobile phones in the UK – not bad for a country of 60 million people. It's no longer a question of naming the people you know who have a mobile – name those who don't have one.

Personally, my mobile is my contact with the outside world. Having lived in almost a dozen different places over the years, and as I'll probably live in a dozen more, a mobile phone is the most convenient way of me keeping in contact with everyone else my age who is constantly on the move. At this stage in my life, living alone, I decided that since most people have my mobile number, it made more sense for me to own a mobile rather than paying line rental each month on a home phone.

Every now and again on a slow news day the media shines a spotlight on a teenager who has gone bankrupt because of an out-of-control phone bill. The problem with mobile phones, and the reason a lot of people get into trouble with them, is that they are essentially a line of credit that has to be repaid each month. More than ever young people, especially, are getting in trouble with humungous bills each month that they struggle to pay.

There's no easy answer for lowering your mobile phone bills – sure I could have put the obvious stuff about hunting down the best deal, but at the end of the day if you need to be told that, maybe you're beyond help. Besides, these days mobile phone carriers lock you into contracts that are expensive to get out of, so that decision usually only comes up every year or two.

Prepaid mobiles alleviate the bill shock factor, although they're better suited to those people who don't use their phones that much, since the majority of these deals have insanely high call costs.

The Barefoot approach to mobile phones is to look at them realistically. You need a phone. You don't need to spend £100 a month on it.

It's true that a lot of people keep getting humungous bills, and have to scrimp and save to pay them off each month, and in doing so make a pact with themselves to lower their bill the next month. Like most people I've racked up some huge monthly bills on my mobile, and have dreaded the bill coming at the end of the month. Also like most people, I have made a pact with myself after I've paid the bloody thing at the end of the month that this next month I'm going to be sensible ...

It doesn't work.

Well not for me, and not for any of the people I've spoken to either. All the best intentions in the world go out the window when there's a minor tragedy that needs to be resolved, you're feeling lonely, that cute boy at the gym grunts in your direction, or you're pissed at the pub and decide to call your friends and tell them how much you love them – for forty-five minutes.

The day I saw the light, was the day that I finally came clean with myself. Much like a dieter at McDonald's, I stopped kidding myself that next month would be any different, and accepted that I have friends, and as a result of this I make calls. Could I save myself money by getting rid of my phone? Yes. Would I ever do it? God no!

I worked out that I was spending roughly £50 a month on phone calls on my £15 a month plan. I then went to my phone company and asked them to find me a package (that fitted into my contract) that allowed me to lower my call costs in exchange for raising my call plan slightly.

I also looked at ways I could change my phone habits which could save me in the long run, like taking advantage of off-peak rates, training myself to text message people instead of calling someone and asking, 'How far away are you?' These few things had a huge impact on my bottom line. The result? My hundred-pound phone bill on a higher call plan each month now only costs me £30. The real problem with mobile phones is the denial game. Most people stick on a twenty-pound plan and pay bills of fifty pounds or more, with the attitude being, next month I'll bring it down.

Face reality people.

If you consistently spend £25 a month on calls, deal with it. If you can accommodate a higher dollar plan as part of your weekly spending plan call your phone carrier and ask them if they can make it cheaper.

The best thing about the world of telecommunications is that the competition is fierce. It's a classic case of the free enterprise system at work. We've taken up mobile phones with vigour and the result has been better (and smaller) handsets, and as competition has set in, lower prices both in handsets and call charges.

Mobile phone usage is here to stay, and you can bet your bottom dollar that call rates will continue to come down as competitors compete for your hard-earned dollar. Let them fight, and take advantage of it so you can win.

Don't be the fall guy

Legally binding contracts are just that—legally binding, and whether you're planning to be the next TV-generated pop star or you're in the market for a mobile phone, reading the fine print of a contract is essential. Consumer groups have been outspoken about some of the tactics mobile phone sellers have been using on young people—'free phones', dodgy plans and terms that lock you in to a plan for up to two years.

It pays not to be pressured into signing anything you don't fully understand. If need be, before you sign a contract, show it to someone independent who can explain it. You can also get the company selling you the phone to detail the major terms of the contract in writing (ask them to sign it) before you sign up. This puts the pressure back on them to detail the fine print and justify any harsh or unreasonable clauses. There's no free lunch, and certainly no such thing as a free phone. Buyer beware.

Different types of debt explained

You'll soon see that different types of debt have the same simple aim – to get you in debt at the highest interest rate possible for as long as possible. The way they do this is different in each case but the outcome is the same – to mess you up financially.

Credit cards

I'm not a fan of credit cards. Since doing *The Barefoot Investor* radio programme, I've met hundreds of people who were in serious shit with credit card debt. It's one of the major reasons people of all ages get into deep financial problems that stop them from achieving the things they want the most.

Total credit card debt in the UK is now around £56 billion, 76 per cent more than in 2000. With a typical interest rate of 2 per cent a month, that means we are collectively shelling out £1.1 billion a month, or £37 million a day, just in interest.

Let's look at credit cards the Barefoot way. Strip away the 'priceless' marketing, the seductive gold card, and the rewards points, and what you have left is a plastic card that allows you to purchase shit you can't afford. In the process you get charged rates that are (at the moment) nearly three times the level of interest that people pay for their mortgages.

Credit card companies work in much the same way as cigarette companies in that they hook you in when you're young with a little balance for emergencies, and then start raising your limit – and before you know it you're in serious debt.

Again, cutting through all the nonsense, credit cards are designed as a short-term loan, by way of a line of credit. Just like any ordinary loan you will one day need to pay it off – although credit card companies are less concerned with you repaying and more focused on getting you to increase your credit limit. Why? Because they are charging you an interest rate that makes them heaps of cash! Why would they ever want you to pay it back?

Let's look at a typical situation that people find themselves in.

While you're studying you have a basic package that gives you cheap banking, a debit card, and a linked credit card with a sensible £500 limit. After you've finished studying you find that your bank is now sending you pre-approved credit card limits, and before you know it you've got a three grand limit on your card, and you're balance is now up around the two grand mark.

Not to worry, all you have to do is to make the minimum repayments, or have a windfall and it'll all be paid off. Let's look at this situation a little closer:

A card-carrying hostage

With £1000 racked up on your card, even at a relatively cheap rate of 16 per cent a year, if you pay back the minimum amount, this is what you are likely to look forward to:

Minimum repayments costing you £25 a month
11 years to pay off the debt
£860 in interest

The worst thing with credit cards is after a while you've got this haemorrhaging balance, but you've got nothing to show for it. Think about it, there's no car, usually no furniture, credit cards are usually used for living expenses. Maybe you had some nice dinners, some good nights out, but usually you've got nothing of value – except for a heap of debt!

When you carry a credit card balance over one month to another there is absolutely no point in looking at any other investment. The point is, most credit cards charge interest rates well above the rate at which even the fastest investments grow. That's why whenever someone asks me what they should do with their money, my first response is always, 'Pay off your cards.' It's the best return you'll likely ever earn.

A consistent 18 per cent return on your money has only been achieved by a few investors throughout history, but that's probably the rate of return that you're giving your credit card company! Of course credit card companies don't want you to pay it back, even the best fund managers in the world can't achieve those results!

Rewards points—smoke and mirrors

A few years ago financial institutions were faced with a problem. Debit cards were starting to grow in popularity – to the detriment of credit cards. Banks were understandably worried. After all, if they can get people to make their purchases on credit, and then hold that balance, they're able to charge huge rates of interest and make serious sums of cash.

Question: How could they convince people to start using credit cards again?

Answer: Introduce reward points – frequent flyer miles, holidays or discounts on big-ticket items, the list goes on and on.

One of the golden principles of the Barefoot Investor is there's no such thing as a free lunch. That's especially true when we're talking about credit card companies offering so called rewards for spending money. Has introducing rewards points remedied the faltering use of credit cards? You betcha! Essentially reward points encourage people to spend more money than they have, to chase rewards that they'll probably never collect.

In most cases reward points don't come cheap. Choosing a credit card with a healthy amount of rewards often means you'll be charged either a higher interest rate, or a higher annual fee, or both. In his book, Graham Hand argues that if a bank charges £100 annual membership fee, you will need to spend £13 000 to gain enough reward points to break even.

All the frequent flyer points in the world aren't going to bring a smile to your face when you can't afford to go anywhere once the plane hits the ground.

I'm leaving on a jet plane—don't know when I'll be back again

A common myth with the cult of credit is the old line that if you're planning a big trip overseas you should pay for it on your credit card and earn a stack of points—the story goes that (depending on the cost of the trip) you should be able to rack up enough points to get you a domestic flight when you return to our fine shores.

When I booked my last overseas trip, I spoke to my travel agent about the pros and cons of paying for it on plastic. Smoke and mirrors again people. She explained that this is an urban myth that rivals the one about the guy who wakes up in an ice-cold bath with no kidneys. She'd been overseas three times that year alone and still hadn't racked up enough points for a domestic flight.

Even though I loathe the carrot that credit card companies offer people in the form of rewards points, there are times when you can screw these guys at their own game when it comes to travelling. If you're planning a big trip overseas, investigate getting a card that has complimentary travel insurance included for cardholders. It could save you pounds that could be better directed towards enjoying a pint of Guinness in Ireland.

As with everything, make sure you read the terms and conditions of the credit card you're applying for. In some cases, the travel insurance linked to the card may not be worth the paper it's written on, and unless you are travelling first class around the world forget the frequent flyer con—with domestic fares currently at rock-bottom prices, you may find the annual fee works out to be more than a domestic fare. As with everything, it pays to read the fine print and get good advice.

What's the answer?

Credit cards should be looked at as a temporary loan of a month or so, and then the amount has to be repaid in full, otherwise you're going to be stung with a ridiculous screw-me interest rate.

If you don't think you'll be able to repay the amount you're charging on your card by the end of the month, you've got to decide whether you really need the thing you're buying. Your banking institution may exhibit the characteristics of a drug dealer trying to get you hooked (on credit). They'll slip a pre-approved credit limit in the mail; they may even ring you and tell you they'll raise your limit 'just in case'. Don't play that game.

Keep your credit limit at a monthly manageable limit, like £250. The most important thing is to make sure that its an amount that can be safely cleared by the end of each month.

Credit-card cred

The smart way of dealing with credit is twofold:

1. Limit your limit
Make sure your credit limit is an amount that you can safely manage to pay off each month without sweating too much.

2. Black is beautiful
Keep your credit card in the black. When you pay off your credit card each month, pay a few pounds extra so that your account is in credit.

Although credit card companies will never admit it, credit providers love to see people who are not only able to meet their repayments, but who can keep their account in the black. This is comparable to bringing an apple for the teacher – your credit rating will love you for it. The other reason this is a great idea is that it trains your mind not only to meet your repayments, but also to make sure that there is a little left over in the account.

If you still want to chase the lure of rewards points, the next time you want to purchase a big-ticket item, top your card up with your own money – that way you can still earn the points (check the fine print), without incurring the debt.

Store cards

Store cards are essentially the same as credit cards, except they're issued in conjunction with a store and often give discounts and benefits to cardholders.

The reason retailers offer credit cards is that they encourage people to shop at their store and spend more money than they ordinarily would because they have been granted additional credit. Secondly, the interest that is charged on store cards is traditionally a lot higher than regular credit cards.

Retailers are in a win-win situation. They effectively loan money (usually in association with a finance company) at ridiculously high rates to people under the proviso that the credit is spent at their stores.

When looked at logically store cards are a waste of time, unless you pay off the balance in full – which research shows most people can't or don't do.

Interest-free offers or 'Buy now with no deposit and nothing to pay till 2006!'

So your version of Rancho Relaxo isn't going to be featured in *Ideal Home* anytime soon, and being a young, upwardly mobile mover and shaker you decide that your mother's lime green hand-me-down couch and the pine coffee table with the wonky leg are just not cutting it anymore. Maybe you could get away with the *Pulp Fiction* poster when you were in second year uni but you're getting older – these days you're less *Home and Away* and more *Friends* and it's time to start accumulating some funky furniture.

Problem. You have no money. Solution, twelve months interest free at your local mega store. After overdosing on *Changing Rooms* reruns you figure that a new couch, a nice coffee table and a dining setting will transform your current abode, and set you back about two grand.

After carefully doing the sums you figure that you can put away £125 each month and have the loan paid off within the twelve months.

Fast forward twelve months and what with the car breaking down, the once-in-a-lifetime Coldplay Concert and a few parking fines, you've still got £500 left to pay off the loan.

Realising that you're going to roll over onto a high interest rate, you once again do your sums and decide that you're going to have to get serious about paying off the loan.

What you weren't aware of when you tools up the interest-free period was that the interest clock has been ticking over each day since you made the purchase. The result is that at day 366, you get hit with twelve months' interest on the whole amount borrowed at rates much higher than credit card interest rates. It's not uncommon for the interest rate to be 20 per cent or more.

The debt cycle starts to get into full swing now because you have to pay off the grand you have outstanding, plus the twelve months interest, plus you're now paying off the total amount at rates that can quickly double the amount of debt you have if you don't pay them off quickly.

Barefoot Investors know that in most things there's no such thing as a free sofa, especially when you've got people offering to give you stuff that you can take home without paying for it in full.

If you enter into an interest-free agreement, you'll find that your bargaining power at the time of purchase will decrease rapidly. With cash in your hip pocket you can negotiate. If you need the interest-free period you're probably going to get the sticker price. Cash is king!

Personal loans

Personal loans are usually offered by banking institutions or credit unions. The difference between, say, a mortgage on a house and a personal loan is how it's secured.

How *secure* are you? This isn't just a question asked by potential suitors trying to find lurv; lending institutions are also in on the game.

A mortgage is a perfect example of a secured loan. It uses the property as the asset to secure the loan, so in the event of you defaulting on your mortgage the lender can sell your house and recoup the money it's owed.

A personal loan is usually unsecured, in that you don't have to put up anything in collateral to get the cash, and in the advent of you going bankrupt the lender has little to no claim on your assets. To compensate lenders for taking the extra risks, the interest rates charged on unsecured loans are higher, usually from 10 per cent to 16 per cent or more, depending on interest rates at the time.

There are only a few reasons you should ever look into taking out a personal loan, such as consolidating all your debts to a lower interest rate (more on that later) or getting hit with a large bill that you have to pay (like an insurance payout), but that's about it.

One of the biggest mistakes people make is financing a holiday through debt – it's short-term gain in exchange for long-term pain. The reason you take holidays is to take a break from everyday

Keep your eyes on the road and your hands on the wheel

Borrowing money for brand new cars is just plain stupid. You're borrowing for something that is rapidly decreasing in value, while at the same time your loan is growing.

However, life is not so black and white, right and wrong. There are extenuating circumstances, and besides, everyone is unique and treading their own path.

Let's say you land a job that requires you to be on the road quite a bit (and doesn't give you a company car), or maybe you land a job that's half an hour away from home and not accessible by public transport.

If you don't have a car you may miss out on the opportunity. If you don't have the cash it may be sensible to take out a small loan to buy a quality second-hand vehicle that will allow you to get to the job and earn some cash.

stresses, and if you finance a holiday through debt the pain starts as soon as you get off the plane. A holiday is much more enjoyable and rewarding if you've earned it.

So repeat after me, 'I will not borrow for anything that falls in value'. If you don't have the cash, don't buy it.

Student loans

The curse of the educated class, student loans is something most university educated people have to deal with – our combined student loan bill has already hit a staggering $10 billion. There is much conjecture as to the merits of paying off the debt. Let's see what all the fuss is about.

Higher education: the chance to grow intellectually, to debate the issues that shape our world, to gain skills that will allow us to become contributing members of society.

Beer and bar nights. Sleeping through lectures. Cramming a semester worth of learning into an afternoon. Wasting time e-mailing friends in the computer labs. Welcome to higher education.

Sleeping through a first-year lecture nursing a hangover from the night before, student loans is probably the last thought to pierce your shaky consciousness. Fail a few units, who cares? The student loan has become a fact of life for many young people. This attitude starts to change when you get out of university and find yourself in gainful employment. University is not free, and that student loan debt will need to be repaid.

If you had parents that were really smart and went to university, you may be shocked to hear that university was once free, just like primary and high school. Unfortunately, times have definitely changed, and as a result of a less stable job market more people are taking the opportunity to get more education. The influx of people going to university has meant that the government can no longer fully subsidise higher education – enter tuition fees and student loans.

Student loan repayments depend on your income. You start repaying after you leave once your income reaches £288 a week, or £15 000 a year. Anything you earn over this amount, 9 per cent of it goes as a loan replayment, collected through the tax system.

The government keeps reminding everyone that with student loans you don't pay interest, which is true, but the debt does rise with the cost of living, usually an increase of about 2–3 per cent a year. What this means is that your debt will be re-rated each year to take inflation into account. So although your student loan debt does not increase because of interest charges, it will still maintain its present value as the years go by.

The government wants its money back sooner rather than later, and offers discounts to those people smart enough to squirrel away enough cash to make a downpayment on their education, although, again these are due to change in the new year.

If you get a windfall from, say, an inheritance or a bonus you can choose to pay off some (or all) of your student loan.

Should I repay my student loan?

One of the questions I am asked most frequently is whether young people should pay off student loans or invest their money somewhere else.

Throughout this book I have made it a point to give advice based on what's worked for me. I've never seen the point of telling people the right thing to do if I haven't put it to the test myself.

I have chosen to pay off my student loan largely because I have analysed my financial choices and the returns I could reasonably expect. In Australia they get a 15 per cent discount on any lump sum paid off a student loan and since it is hard to make a return like that consistently on the stock market, it makes sense to do that. In the UK, there is no discount like this so there is no point busting a gut to do the same, especially if you have other high-interest debts.

If for some reason you come across enough money to clear most, if not all of your student loan debt off in one hit (winning the lottery or receiving an inheritance), you should certainly consider doing it, if of course you have no other higher interest debts.

If you don't have the cash to put a seriously big dent in your debt in the one hit, you're probably better off using what little savings you have to start a regular investing plan.

Paying off your debt— an action plan

The Barefoot debt elimination plan is alarmingly simple. Other financial types may have complicated formulas and week-by-week plans on getting your debts under control.

Bugger that. You got yourself in debt, now it's time to get yourself out.

Moloko says no time like the present. I agree. By directing all your cash towards getting out of debt, by making it as real and as painful as possible, until every last cent has been repaid, you'll develop true character.

If you can direct everything to paying off the money you owe, you'll not only pay off your debt quicker than you ever thought possible, you'll have developed the traits that will ensure that once you're finally out of debt you'll have the shills to reach your goals faster.

In the words of the immortal Gordon Gecko from the movie *Wall Street*, 'Christmas is over and business is business'. If you ever want to get ahead, if you ever want to be able to achieve the financial goals that you've set for yourself, you've got to pay off your debts.

Regardless of your situation, it's time to put all your debt on the table, take a realistic look at all of it, and determine the quickest way out. The sooner it's sorted the better.

The debt pyramid

One of the problems with being in debt is that it seems to hit you from all sides. There's long-term debt like car loans, personal loans, credit cards, even money borrowed from mates – they all need to be repaid, but instead of getting them out of the way, human nature tells us that most people end up like your grandma at a disco – too stunned to move.

Introducing the debt pyramid

So deceptively simple even Jessica Simpson could understand, comes the time-honoured debt pyramid. The basic premise of the debt pyramid is that you pay off the debt with the highest interest rate first, and then move down the pyramid until it's all paid off.

The pyramid is divided into three separate sections: high-interest debt, loans from friends, and long-term debt.

Put all your debts on the table, including anything you've borrowed from family or friends, and rank them by:

- The interest you're being charged
- The total amount outstanding

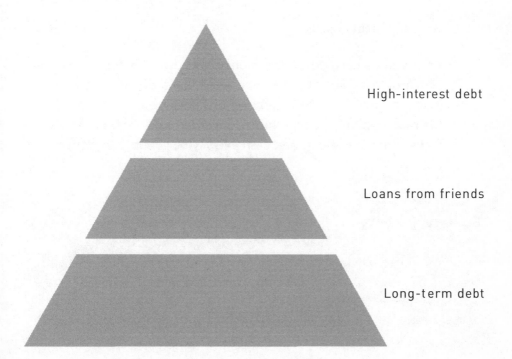

High-interest debt

Loans from friends

Long-term debt

High-interest debt: Include the highest interest rate debts that you're paying on any of your loans. For most people it will be their credit card loans, cash advances, loans from a finance company, or an interest-free time bomb. Rank them from highest to lowest.

Loans from friends: Write down all the cash you've borrowed from your friends. Those IOUs add up, and if you think your mates have long forgotten, ask yourself whether you've ever forgotten when someone owes you money. If you've ever been in the situation of lending (or borrowing) money from a friend, you'll no doubt have noticed that it usually puts considerable strain on the friendship. The relationships you have with your friends are the most important things in your life. To jeopardise them because of a few quid is downright stupid. Pay them back and earn their respect.

Long-term debts: These include car loans, personal loans, and student loans.

Write in the details in the debt pyramid so that you can get a snap-shot of the money you owe.

Get out of debt quickly

After you've detailed all the money you owe, it's time to get pro-active by paying it off. This may seem like a daunting task, but by following the pyramid technique of knocking off each debt from the most expensive to the more longer-term debt, you'll be able to focus your time, energy and cash into saying goodbye to them one by one.

Go Jerry, Go Jerry ...

If you're prone to watching daytime television you may have noticed all the finance companies that run ads through such highbrow programmes as Jerry Springer and CSI.

These ads target people who are in trouble with debt and offer miracle cures to reconsolidate your debts and get you out of trouble. Some of these companies may well be reputable, in the same way that the guests on Jerry Springer may be reputable, but I would still advise people to stay away from them. Most of the time the only people they help is themselves, by charging outrageous fees. Dealing with these companies may get you in deeper trouble than the guests on Jerry Springer.

Debt consolidation

A good financial rule of thumb is that repayments on personal debt (excluding student loans) shouldn't amount to more than 15 per cent of your weekly take-home pay. If you find yourself in this boat, or you have large amounts of debt in the high-interest category, you may want to think about debt consolidation.

Essentially this is taking out a loan to cover all your debts and then paying off the loan with structured payments from your bank. Most people view debt consolidation as the easy way out: it's kind of like what liposuction is to exercise – an admission of defeat.

The advantage is that it may well decrease the average amount of interest that you are being charged, and give you the discipline of regular repayments since the lending institution (usually a bank) often takes the repayments by direct debiting your pay – you do have a job don't you?

Having all your debts put in one (large) basket can also ease the paralysis that often occurs when you have debts all over the place.

If you're thinking about debt consolidation, book in and see an independent financial adviser, or better still speak to the Citizens Advice Bureau or an organisation like Credit Action that offers financial counselling. See the website directory at the back of the book for more information. They will be able to give you impartial advice on the best course of action.

Bankruptcy

Let's say that you've done the debt pyramid, and it came as no surprise that your debt situation is completely out of control. Your income, or lack thereof, hasn't a hope of paying off all your debts anytime soon. You're pretty sure your credit card company has a hit man looking for you.

You've thought about debt consolidation, but even if you scoop all your debts into one basket you're not going to have enough money to make the repayments, and the autographed Milli Vanilli single *Blame It on the Rain* that you have been holding onto as an investment hasn't exactly risen in value the way you thought it would.

If you're in this situation, I don't need to tell you what a stress being seriously in debt is. But before you flee the country and lie low on the Costa del Crime, there are options available to you besides the B word, BANKRUPTCY.

The B word

Bankruptcy should be the last resort for anyone with serious amounts of debt, and it should go without saying that before you tread this path you should have investigated all other options with your financial counsellor.

People talk about bankruptcy these days as if it's a get-of-jail-free card – your debts are erased, you're given a slap on the wrist, and then you start again. While this may be true for some high-flying businessmen, the reality of going bankrupt isn't nearly as straightforward for most of us.

When you are declared bankrupt you must surrender all of your money and assets to a court appointed trustee, who gains control over your money and your assets and has the power to sell them to pay off your debts. For the period that you're bankrupt you'll be refused credit, and you'll have to surrender your passport – which means you aren't able to leave the country without court approval, although you're broke, so a holiday isn't going to be on the top of your 'to do' list anytime soon.

And that's only the start of it. Bankruptcy may be a convenient way of wiping your slate clean, but it comes at a considerable cost. Details of your bankruptcy are kept on your credit file for seven years, and kept on public record *forever*.

Being registered as a bankrupt can have a far-reaching impact on you in later life. You will find it hard to obtain credit in the future, and it may limit your choice of career.

When you're young with the rest of your life ahead of you, apart from appearing in an unauthorised 'home video' distributed via the web, having a black mark on your name is the last thing you want.

Checking your credit history

Everyone has a history. Maybe you're a bit of a straight shooter in matters of the heart and agree with the whole monogamy thing. Others may spend a bit of time sowing their wild oats, and in the process develop quite a chequered history.

Whatever the case, the things we do when we are single and care-free tend to catch up with us at some stage in later life. The same goes with credit.

Ever wondered if Big Brother is watching you? He sure is, but there's no actually three of them. The Big Brothers are called Experian, Equifax and CallCredit. These guys are a central intelligence agency that holds information on anyone who has a loan or credit card, and that's pretty much all of us. Lenders can use this to verify your credit worthiness, meaning that if a potential lender sees something on your profile that makes them nervous, the chances of you getting credit reduces accordingly. Think credit cards, car loans, store loans (gasp) and home loans.

These guys not only keep your all-important credit rating, they also document every application or inquiry that you have made for finance in the last five years, as well as records of court judgments against you, and any bankruptcy details.

Not stressed yet? Well how about if I tell you that institutions can also add stuff to your file if you fail to pay bills?

Now I have your attention, I'll point out that in order for an institution to record this on your credit file it has to be something pretty major, but in this crazy technological world that we live in, mistakes do happen and when it's something as serious as our credit rating you want to make sure everything's kosher.

If you've had troubles in the past it is essential that you find out exactly what is on your file. If you are applying for credit you should always be upfront with the lending institution because chances are they'll find out anyway, and without a good credit rating you need all the goodwill they can throw at you.

If this is starting to sound spooky, there is an upside. If you are denied credit on the basis of what's contained on your file, the lender will advise you to get a copy of your file so you can verify the details. Credit reference agencies by law, must allow you access to your credit record.

Credit reference agencies have phone services and web sites where, by paying £2, you can get to a paper copy of your credit file.

Once you get your report, read through it carefully and if you believe it contains any mistakes, you have the right to have them corrected. A bad credit rap will follow you around longer than that Jason Donovan mullet you had when you were 14 ... so it pays to ensure that your file is up to date and correct.

4

Work Your Mojo

MOJO INVESTING

Step 4 of the Barefoot Plan is where things really start cooking.

The three previous chapters have involved you setting down goals that will inspire you, getting your spending plan sorted, and paying off any debt that may be lurking in your bottom draw.

These steps have built a solid foundation to create wealth on your terms. Now it's time to take the third high-yielding account you set up as part of Step 2— your Mojo account, and turbo charge your returns via investing.

By sticking with the mojo plan, and directly debiting a percentage of your wage into the account YOU WILL BECOME A MILLIONAIRE in good time.

Let's say you get your first job at eighteen, and decide to start contributing £500 a year into a Mojo account earning a (historical average) of 10 per cent a year. At age thirty you take a trip on a boat and end up on *Gilligan's Island* where you stay with the gang until the captain works out how to get you back to the mainland thirty years later.

You're pretty pleased that you're back in civilisation (Gilligan was getting a little too friendly with the captain for your liking) but fear that because you haven't invested a penny since you were thirty you'll be broke.

The £6500 that you invested from 18 to 30 has now grown to £233 000.

This story illustrates the power of the Barefoot Plan, and the power of Mojo Money.

Remember:
- You don't need a lot of money to make your million.
- You don't need expert knowledge on what stock to buy, or what the economy is doing.

- You don't need to spend hours keeping track of your investments.
- You can get started with as little as £250 and continue with just £1 a day!
- All the tools to get a Mojo account are outlined in this step and can be set up within an hour.

As we grow older one of our biggest concerns is a lack of money. By setting up your Mojo account today you'll have the peace of mind that as you get older your money is growing faster than you can earn it!

My humble beginnings

Do kids invest? Not unless they're child prodigies like Doogie Houser MD pulling in a doctor's wage. I was no child genius, but my future career (obsession) was ingrained at an early age.

It's often said that parents try to live their lives through their children. One night over a few beers with a group of mates we realised how true that was. Steve told us how as a kid his father was always dragging him out of bed on a Sunday morning to help him tinker with the family car. Little did he know that his father was guiding him towards his future career as a mechanic. By his own admission, those Sunday mornings went a long way to shaping his interest in 'heavy metal'.

The same thing happened to me. My old man grew up in rural Australia and never had access to a formal education but, to his credit, he became a successful businessman whose education came largely from trial and error. Even though he has no letters after his name, he has always been passionate about investing and, much like Steve's dad, from an early age he cultivated and nurtured that same interest in me.

When I was about eleven one of my jobs was to open the mail for my father's business, sorting out the bills from the cheques. Every so often a thick envelope from BHP (a big Australian mining company) would come across the desk. Dad would sit down and explain to me that he owned part of one of the world's most successful resource companies, and that when they made money they shared it with him. Now every kid sees their father as a hero when they're young, and the idea that my dad was a part owner in a huge company blew my little mind, which as I now know was all part of his master plan.

One day my father came to me with a proposition: if I worked for him doing odd jobs after school he'd pay me an allowance, and within a few months I'd be able to buy my very own share of BHP. As time went on I swept floors, made hand deliveries and washed windows until I had enough money to purchase one share in BHP. It mattered not that it was my father 'selling' me the share, and therefore there was no official legal ownership. (Hey, I was eleven, what the hell did I know about securities law?) Yet each day my father would open the paper and show me how to look up the share price of BHP. Sometimes it would rise, sometimes fall, but it didn't matter – the seed had been planted.

Through my early teenage years I was always working part-time at something – selling hot dogs in the local park, leaflet deliveries on my BMX, and being the water boy for the local Sunday league football team, mainly little one-offs that supplemented my parental endowment, which certainly wasn't enough wonga to live at large.

The employment law in Australia stipulated that you had to be fourteen and nine months before you could start work. So to the day, at the spritely age of fourteen and nine months I entered the job market. I entered the world of gainful employment at Safeway supermarket.

I started my illustrious career working in the delicatessen of my local Safeway. Much to my dismay I was the only male member of the 'team' and was forced to wear a paper hat and slice cold cuts for roughly £3.50 an hour – not the type of money that was going to see me challenge the Sunday Times rich list any time soon.

Let's get one thing straight – I hated that job. From slicing salami to stuffing chickens this job sucked, big time. Making things worse was the continual parade of friends who would come to the supermarket to see me in my paper hat and bright red bow tie ... I was one bitter and twisted young man.

As the weeks went by I noticed that indeed my little bank balance was starting to creep up. After all, I'd yet to develop a penchant for alcohol, fine dining or the Beastie Boys. I was fifteen! The only expenses I had were the occasional school canteen splurges.

One of my regular customers was Charlie, a financial adviser. He encouraged me to take my stash of cash and invest it in a mutual managed fund. My father had continued to fan the flames of my interest in investing so I decided to give it a go. I stopped by Charlie's office one day after school and picked up a heap of pamphlets on different managed funds to choose where to park my cash.

Let someone else do the hard work

Managed fund: pooling your money with other investors, and having an uptight Porsche-driving fund manager invest the proceeds on your behalf, for which they charge a fee (which explains the Porsche). They'll go grey making the hard decisions, so you don't have to.

Charlie offered some conservative suggestions on which managers I should use, and what type of investments I should consider. Unfortunately Charlie had yet to realise that a fifteen-year-old knows more about practically everything than anyone on the face of the planet.

The way I chose my fund was probably how most people do: I looked at the past performances of all the funds and chose the one that had achieved the highest return over the last couple of years.

The fund that I chose was a 'special situations fund', which was really a fancy name to describe the fact that the guys running this fund tried to exploit situations that people didn't expect: droughts, floods, a CEO resigning, gold price going up, you name it, these guys bet on it. Now in the previous few years there had been quite a few 'special situations', but as Murphy's Law says, the moment I put my hard earned in, their special situations turned into pretty bloody ordinary situations. The only special situation I was in after a year was that 30 per cent of my cash had evaporated! I was pissed off. How could these clowns have lost my money?

Although I didn't appreciate it at the time, I learnt a good lesson. I formed several new investment rules for myself as a result of that debacle, the first being never invest in anything you don't understand. To be truthful, I had no idea what the managers were doing with my money, what methodology they were using, or even what a 'special situation' was. I wasn't investing. I was gambling on these guys making me money, for all I knew they could have been smoking crack and investing the proceeds on number eight at the dog track.

A short while after this my high school commerce teacher announced that our class was to participate in a national schools stock market game. Contestants were given a mythical £25 000 to invest on the share market and were ranked each week by the size of their portfolio. The winner was the person who was able to turn their original £25 000 into the most money at the end of ten weeks.

As luck would have it, I was one of the best performers for the game, with the focus being on the word luck. On reflection, the thing that annoys me about the game is that it teaches students exactly how not to invest. The game is predicated around picking the best stocks over a two month period – and considering no-one in the last thousand or so years has ever been able to consistently pick the right stocks, this game had more to do with gambling than investing.

Gambling and investing are often lumped together as if they mean

Gambling = Day Trading = Mug Punter

Back in the dotcom boom thousands of people from all over the world turfed in their nine to five jobs to become 'traders'. They sat at home on their computers with online brokerage accounts (often in their Y fronts) and traded in and out of predominantly tech stocks. The market was booming and fortunes were being made ... Well someone was making a fortune, but history showed it wasn't the day traders, most of whom ended up losing most of their cash.

the same thing, but only by people who don't have a clue. You hear people talk about a big win they had by trading shares. A close cousin of this story is the one about getting lucky on the fruit machines.

Gambling is entrenched in our national psyche, and when we talk about trading shares we don't call it gambling – it's given a more respectable name, 'speculating'. Whereas gambling conjures the image of a middle-aged chain-smoking fruit machine player, speculating has an air of mystique – it's exciting, dynamic and it requires thought. In all my years as a broker, I've never met anyone who has made their fortune by trading the market.

Unfortunately 'Wealth 101' isn't offered in schools. It should be. What follows is another invaluable lesson.

The reason you will become a millionaire:
—compound interest (the eighth wonder of the world)

Are you in a comfy chair? Have you locked yourself away from your TV/mother/girlfriend/ boyfriend/wife/husband/neighbour/dog? Excellent.

What you're about to read is the number one reason you have the ability to tread your own path. If you understand and then use this information you won't have to wear a white coat to work for the next forty years to become wealthy, and you won't even have to get to the last question on Who *Wants To Be a Millionaire* – you will be a millionaire. And the cherry on top? It requires very little work on your behalf.

Ever heard the phrase 'time is money'? What it's referring to is the power of compound interest. Essentially, compound interest is the accumulation of interest on interest. Let's do the mathematics.

If you put £100 into a term deposit paying 5 per cent a year, after a year you will earn £5 in interest, leaving you with a total of £105. If you choose not to spend the £5, and instead put the £105 in for another year in the fixed term deposit at 5 per cent, you'll now have £110.25 after the second year. Put the £110.25 in for another year and you'll have £115.75.

Am I being sadistic? I lured you in with talk of riches, of getting paid to do nothing and all I've given you is maths and a definition that could have come out of a 1970s' textbook!

Here's one of the great conundrums of finance. It's all in the wrapping. Before you throw the book down in disgust, let me take the maths and the explanation and see if I can use these time-honoured principles in an example that makes sense.

It's the summer of 1973 and two university roommates, Sarah and Linda, finally graduate.

Sarah finds the pottery major she took as part of her arts degree hasn't really helped her career prospects, and takes up a job as a secretary earning a tiny wage. Linda has graduated with top-class honours in law and is accepted into a high-paying position with a prominent law firm.

Sarah is worried that she'll never get ahead because she's getting paid half what Linda is, and therefore diligently decides to scrape together £2000 a year and invests it in a managed fund that returns on average 10 per cent a year.

Linda on the other hand decides its time to start rewarding herself now she's a highly paid lawyer, having spent years scraping by as a student. She's a retail therapy type of gal and blows all her cash, living from one generous pay cheque to the next.

Cut ten years into the future and it's 1983. Sarah decides to stop investing and start spending her cash on the requisite must have 80s' gear – shoulder-padded power suits, hair gel, a betamax video player and a groovy Michael Jackson 'Thriller' zipper jacket – and consequently breaks free from her regular investing habits and never invests another penny.

Linda on the other hand decides that ten years of being a shopaholic hasn't left her with anything of much value and decides to start investing £2000 a year into the same fund that Sarah's money is in.

Cut to the present: Sarah and Linda, now both aged in their early fifties, meet up and compare holdings. Linda has now deposited £40 000 over the last twenty years, which has grown to just over $125 000.

Sarah has only invested half of what Linda has, and hasn't invested a single cent for nearly twenty years. Her current balance is £230 000 almost twice that of Linda's. Even if Linda keeps contributing £2000 each year she'll never catch up to Sarah. Simply put, Sarah has let the magic of time compound her interest longer than Linda. The cruel conclusion to this story is that even if Linda keeps contributing £2000 each year she'll never catch up to Sarah.

The Rule of 72

There's a formula you use to figure out compound interest. Now before your eyes glaze over and you skip this section, I've trained eight-year-olds to do complex compounding calculations in their head using this formula.

It's called the Rule of 72. and it's a surprisingly easy method of working out how long it will take for your invested money to double.

The way it works is by dividing 72 by the rate of return. The answer is the number of years it will (approximately) take your money to double. How long will it take to double your money at 10 per cent? Seventy-two divided by 10 = 7.2 years to double your money.

I know many of you will find it hard to believe that mathematics could be so easy, but it is! Try it at your next party. Nothing is sexier than a girl who can do complex financial calculations in her head. And boys, forget about the pheromones – bust out some compounding calcs and you'll be leaving with her in no time.

When I explain the analogy of Sarah and Linda, people often find it creates more questions than it answers – questions you're probably asking yourself right now!

Let's use the example of a bank account. Each month you receive interest on your total balance. If you don't withdraw the interest you received, and instead let it be added to your original balance, the next month's interest payment will be paid on both your starting balance plus the first interest payment.

To make compounding work for us, we want a high return so our money grows bigger each time interest is paid. Got it?

Question: Sounds good, but I don't know anything about investing.

Answer: All the information you need to be 'Sarah' is contained within this book – and it doesn't require hours spent each week analysing companies, or complicated lingo.

Question: Investing sounds great, but you need heaps of cash to get started – I've got none!

Answer: You will if you follow the plan of depositing 10 per cent of your pay into your Mojo account. With a little of my help you'll soon be effortlessly playing with the big boys – without needing the big bucks. They come later ...

Question: I'm depressed. This is great advice for people in there twenties, but I'm forty, I've left it too late!

Answer: The underlying lesson that compounding interest teaches us is to start investing – the sooner the better. Obviously compound interest is something that can have a huge impact on the bottom line of any young person who's savvy enough to get their financial situation sorted before they get to the age of appreciating red wine for the flavour and watching TV just for *Panorama* and *Question Time*, however the effects of compound interest are not ageist.

Question: I understand compounding – it means I'll be rich when I'm old. I'm never going to get old – varicose veins, balding, hip replacements; it's just not for me. I don't want a plan for when I'm old, I want one for right now goddamn it!

Answer: If you follow this plan you'll be rich when you're old. Big deal. I don't live my life on a delayed-payment plan, and I don't expect you to either.

People often come to me saying that they want to make a lot of money, actually they're usually wanting me to make them lots of money. I tell these people that they don't really want to make lots of money. I then explain that money is simply a piece of paper (well plastic these days), which on its own means nothing. Of course by this stage they think I've totally lost my marbles.

People don't want money for money's sake. They're chasing what they believe money will give them, be it power, prestige, comfort, pleasure – whatever it is they believe having money means to them.

Money allows us to live life on our terms. It allows us to walls tall through life without needing to look for a handout of any kind. Sure, if you follow the plan one day you'll have enough money to buy the toys you want.

Stress is a killer. What do most people stress about? Money, of course, or to be precise, the lack of it in their lives. As you move through life you'll be in the unique situation of seeing your money grow into something substantial – eliminating your financial woes, leaving you to spend your time focusing on things that are more important than pounds and pence.

The Gasping Millionaire

Let's say you meet a new 'friend' – a special friend – as in one whose sexual magnetism can do what the threat of cancer, and your parents haven't been able to do – get you to quit your 30-a-day smoking habit. Let's suppose your special friend has read this book and encourages you to put the £50 you normally spend on ciggies into a fully functioning Mojo account that we're about to get into. We'll assume that you earn an average 10 per cent return a year, and that the power of lurv means that you keep putting the ciggie money in each week. Here's what you will accumulate:

1 year	=	£2528
2 years	=	£5309
3 years	=	£8368
4 years	=	£11 733
5 years	=	£15 434
10 years	=	£40 292
20 years	=	£144 797
30 years	=	£415 859
40 years	=	**£1 118 92**

What are your options?

What does investing mean to you? Depending on your level of enthusiasm, your reaction to the word 'investing' will either pique your interest or it will make you dry retch. If you're like most people though, it's probably something that's around number nine on your to-do list. Something you should get around to doing, just ahead of stopping smoking and giving up the Friday night sessions that invariably leave you with a hangover to greet the start of a weekend.

When you think about it we invest in things whether we are conscious of it or not. We make investments in our relationships, in our friendships, even our careers. There is no cash changing hands (usually!) – moreover we invest our time, energy, and thoughts and feelings. The people who 'invest' in the things that are important to them are those who are undoubtedly the most successful – be it in relationships, careers or money. Granted, I'm going a little Oprah Winfrey here, but it's the same concept applied in a different way.

Straight from the hip, investing has received a bad rap. It's fair to say that most of us have an incorrect view of what investing really is. It's not our fault, we've been bought up on a diet of television and movies that show frantic traders in multicoloured jackets waving their hands around like Eddy Murphy on speed, or worse – movies like *Wall Street* that depict the testosterone-fuelled greed where fortunes are made (and lost) in the blink of an eye. This side of investing does exist, in the same way that Paris Hilton does have an acting career (in home movies and blockbusters). In reality most investors are ordinary everyday people like you and me.

I'm a stockbroker and my job entails directing people's cash into long-term assets that will increase in value over time. There you have it. No panic-stricken phone calls, no trading, just lock, load and forget.

The search

There are a million and one 'investments' being touted out there. From savings bonds to Russian brides – how can you distinguish which is going to make you money, or lose it for that matter? Early on in my career I worked it out.

Up until the point where I lost some of my hard-earned, like most teenagers, I believed that people over the age of thirty had no idea what they were talking about. I also had enough testosterone to believe that I could master the markets – although my dwindling portfolio was disagreeing with me. I realised that it might be time for me to rethink my strategy.

I was determined to reverse my fortunes, so I embarked on a mission to learn everything I could about investing. I quizzed knowledgeable stockbrokers and financial planners, had long talks with my father, and read anything I could get my hands on about investment.

My journey of learning about investing had parallels with my attempts to learn about the opposite sex. At the start of each endeavour I would learn something, say that girls like flowers and I would think to myself, 'right, now I understand women'. Same thing went for investments. I'd learn something that made sense to me, and then (much like women) I'd have another experience that totally contradicted my previous beliefs.

Everywhere I read I was confronted with stuff on diversification, betas, ratios, compounding formulas and yields. Just as confusing, nearly every book I read had different opinions on what was the best investment, and how to make money. It seemed everyone was pushing a different way to invest.

I'm a firm believer that every topic can be stripped down to bare logic. Why should investing be any different? In fact it's not, it's just that when it comes to money people go a little mad. It's really quite simple. When you invest you are essentially putting your savings into an 'asset' with the desire to make more money.

But just what is an asset? Determined to find out I started quizzing experts on what an asset was to them. The answers I got were: shares, the family home, tracker funds, silver, junk bonds, options, futures, gold, fixed interest, cash. Then there are people who talked about art, stamps, antique furniture and classic cars.

What a nightmare! With all these conflicting opinions from so-called experts, how could I ever find what was the best investment for me? The rule I learnt, and now follow, is: an asset is something that puts money in your pocket.

Looking at this I quickly saw that antiques (of any description) pay no dividends, rent, or return of any kind – so too with art, classic cars, stamps, eighties Ra-Ra skirts, or even gold bullion. When I explain this to people, invariably someone will counter with – 'but I know someone who made a killing investing in art!'

Again, there are only two ways to make money out of an asset:

1. Via the income it generates (putting cash back in your pocket)
2. By the value of the asset increasing

In the book *Motivated Money* author Peter Thornhill calls this second type of investing the 'greater fool theory'. What he is getting at is that because these types of investments don't generate an income they rely on just one thing to make money – a 'greater fool' paying more money for the 'asset' than was originally paid to purchase it.

The process of selecting an investment was becoming clearer. I now understood that if I wanted to I could buy artwork that I was inspired by, drive a classic car if that's what got me going, even fill my (share house) with antiques, but when it came to making money there were only three main assets that generate income – property, which generates income from rent, cash or fixed interest that generates income from the interest that borrowers pay, and shares in a business that pay dividends (a fancy term for sharing the profits).

Risky business

After my initial hammering from my 'special situation' debacle, it tools me a while to part with the cash I'd saved up. Now, bearing in mind I'd read all about investing, I understood that if I invested for the long term compound interest would make me a wealthy person, and I'd read practically everything I could get my hands on about investments – but still, this was different, I was investing my own money! What if I lost 30 per cent like last time? Worse, what if I lost the lot? Risk is one of the hardest things for investors to grasp.

There are unwritten rules that each of us understand: stay away from your mate's sister, double denim is for nerds, and going home for a 'coffee' after a romantic date isn't actually about drinking coffee. In the world of investing the unwritten rule that all investors must understand is the higher the risk, the higher the return. Let's have a look at how this plays out with our 'income-generating assets'.

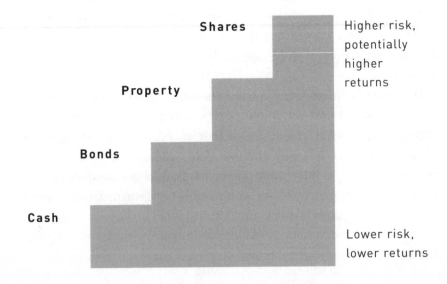

Cash: Includes the stuff in your wallet (doh!), your everyday bank account, savings accounts, and cash management trusts, which are essentially savings accounts for people with a few thousand dollars. For all of these products, you get paid via the interest the bank pays you – which is usually bugger all. It's the safest place to stash your cash, and because of this it offers the lowest returns.

Bonds: Let's move up a step and assume a little more risk by getting into a bit of bondage, sorry, bonds, which in effect involves you lending your money to the government or a company for a set time, and they 'cross their heart and hope to die' that they'll pay it back with interest, which is how you get paid. It's a little riskier – the company you loaned it to could go broke and not be able to pay the money back. Of course, this rarely happens, but it's still not out of the realm of possibility. Anyway, if you're giving your money over for a set period of time, and if there's even a slight chance you may lose your dough, you're certainly going to want to get a better return than people who are putting their money in the bank. A little more risk equals a slightly higher return.

Property: As we've discussed you generate your cash from property via rent, but you can also make money by the asset appreciating in value – just look at the property market in London. When you invest in property you can either buy a place and rent it out to a group of stoned students or you can join other investors by becoming part of a trust that invests in office towers, shopping centres, casinos – the list goes on and on, but I think you get the drill. It's investing in commercial buildings as opposed to residential homes. There are considerable risks involved in property, and it's not just the problem of finding a tenant. Property isn't something you can trade (although people have tried their best lately), mainly because of the drawn-out process of finding a buyer, arranging finance and settling the property usually takes about three months. Higher risk, potentially higher return.

Shares: We've arrived at my favourite asset – the sexy world of shares! When I talk about shares, I'm talking about being a part-owner in a company or, by pooling your money with other investors and letting someone do the investing for you, a managed fund. Just like property, there are two ways to make money out of shares. The first is when a company shares some of its profits with you (which is called a dividend), or in the case of a managed fund a distribution of profits from the manager. Small technicality: sometimes companies don't make profits (or choose not to share their profits) and some-times managers don't make profits either. The second way you make money out of shares is by the price going up, or in the case of a managed fund the basket of shares the manager holds goes up in value. Shares go up, shares go down, shares go all over the place.

Investing in the stock market involves assuming higher risk again, but guess what? The expected potential returns are higher than that of comparable investments.

The higher the risk you assume usually correlates with a higher return. It's simple logic. If there's a chance you could lose all your cash, you want to be rewarded for assuming more risk with the potential of higher returns.

Everything we do contains some element of risk. Inflation is a risk. How so? Well, with inflation running at a historical 4 per cent a year in twenty years the real value of your money isn't going to be worth that much. Remember back in the first chapter where I spoke about my Dad purchasing a beer for 10 pence?

With so much risk out there it's easy to take the view that you've worked hard to sock away your savings and you don't want to risk a penny. This isn't a very smart move. Remember Sarah? She turned £20 000 worth of her savings into a managed fund and thirty years later it turned into nearly a quarter of a million pounds!

As Barefoot Investors we define investing in anything that we don't fully understand as risky. I have known people who know very little about what they're investing in. That's not only risky, it's plain stupid!

As rational, intelligent people we need to start looking at not only the riskiness of different investments, but also the other side of the coin – not assuming enough risk, and therefore having your investments eroded over time by inflation, or coming up short and not achieving your goals.

People tend to think to be a successful investor you must have an innate ability to pick the next hot managed fund or stock that's going to make it huge. Wrong! The real definition of a successful investor is someone who understands why they're investing in the first place, appreciates the returns that they can expect, and has a realistic game plan based on historical averages to achieve them. Let's look at some of those returns on different types of investments over time.

As you can see by the table opposite, each different asset class has its time in the sun at some point. Sadly though, no-one can accurately pick which one will perform best over the next year. Sometimes shares may be the flavour of the month, while next year property might be the prom queen and the year after that cash may be sitting at the top of the heap.

A bloke by the name of Harry Markowitz found that the bulk of an investor's return doesn't come from chasing the next big thing, but rather from the appropriate mix of asset classes (shares, property, fixed interest, cash) you invest in within the portfolio. He even got a Nobel Prize for his efforts. Top work Harry.

Spread yourself around

Managed funds allow you with only a small amount of money to gain exposure to each investment class. As Harry said, the bulk of your returns come from the spread of asset classes you invest in.

No-one knows which investment class is going to perform the best in the following year – by having a stake in all of them you spread (and lower) your risk.

Real annual returns for major asset classes

	Cash	UK Govt. Bond	UK Shares	US Shares	US Govt. Bond
1960–1969	1.8%	−1.1%	4.9%	6.5%	−2.4%
1970–1979	−3.6%	−4.1%	−1.3%	−0.5%	−2.5%
1980–1989	5.1%	7.1%	15.5%	10.3%	9.8%
1990–1999	4.3%	9.7%	14.4%	17.8%	6.1%
2000–2004	2.0%	2.4%	−4.6%	−0.9%	5.3%
1960–2004	1.9%	2.5%	5.9%	6.3%	2.8%
1904–2004	1.1%	1.9%	6.0%	7.1%	2.3%

Source: Barclays Capital

The asset choice for the long term is shares. The old saying of 'be an owner not a loaner' still holds true. Essentially, that means that there are greater returns to be made in owning a business than in lending it money.

You may notice that I haven't mentioned shares before – you may also notice that shares have historically beaten the pants off every other investment *over the long term.*

As my past girlfriends will no doubt agree, like many guys in their mid-twenties, I have 'issues' with commitment. Maybe it's the threat of settling down, the horror of a white picket fence and barbecues on Sunday; maybe it's sharing a toothbrush, or maybe it's facing the fact that I'll never get the opportunity to sleep with a supermodel, but in any event, the C word sends shivers up my spine.

The only thing I do commit to is my stock market investments. The higher the risk you assume, the higher the return. Over the long term, investing in the most successful businesses in the country (and the world) has proved to be the best performing asset class, with the emphasis squarely *over the long term.*

Becoming a stock jock

We've all experienced moments when we've been somewhere and thought, 'the people who own this product/service must be absolutely raking it in'. The deal with investing is that the biggest, brightest and most successful companies are yours to invest your money in. Nothing had changed since my father explained to me about investing: 'I am part-owner in one of the best companies in the world, and they share their profits with me.'

Warren B, the original Regulator

I take my cues from the best investors of all time, so I make no apologies about sounding like I'm a bit queer eye for the straight guy over Warren Buffett, one of the greatest investors in the world and a true Barefooter. Warren doesn't drive a Ferrari, and still lives in the same house he bought when he was in his twenties, which isn't that strange except when you realise he's made over seventy billion dollars through investing. Because of that I choose to get my advice from him, rather than a newspaper ad with a bloke standing in front of a Ferrari offering to sell me the 'secrets' to wealth creation.

Warren's fond of saying, 'Investment is simple, but not easy'. Warren has made billions of dollars, but not by investing in high-technology shares, being a master trader, or investing in 'hot share tips'.

He made his fortune by investing in companies like Coca-Cola, McDonald's, and Gillette (as in, 'the best a man can get'). When asked why he'd invested in Gillette, Warren commented, 'I sleep easy knowing that a couple of billion people wake up each morning and need to shave'.

Up until a few years ago Warren was like most old blokes – totally useless with anything involving a keyboard. So when the dotcom boom was in full swing Warren sat it out on the bench – not buying one share (even though fortunes were being made). He didn't understand computers so he didn't invest. Simple logic we should all follow.

Invest in what you know

My first investment was a classic case of putting my money into something that I had little idea about. In a crushing case of irony, if I had invested in something I did know, like Woolworths, where I was working, my initial £500 would be worth £3000 today!

In the best selling book *One Up on Wall Street* author Peter Lynch, who just happens to be one of the best performing fund managers over the last twenty years, says, 'Twenty years in this business convinces me that any normal person using the customary 3 per cent of the brain can pick stocks just as well, if not better than the average Wall Street expert.'

He also argues that 'the amateur investor has numerous built-in advantages' that should be exploited. According to Lynch, because we are all consumers, often we can pick up on a trend long before it hits the radar of professional investors, who spend the bulk of their day pouring over charts and the financial pages. Take my example. I was working at Safeway supermarket, and at the time I could see that we were beating the pants off our main rival. Why then didn't I put some of my hard-earned into a company that I understood? Therein lies the difference between investing and gambling.

Where I live, in Australia we pride ourselves on knowing the form, be it horse racing, football or cricket. Is there a crossover between keeping up on the form of your favourite football team and watching companies you want to invest in? Lynch argues that each of us has a special interest, which is a potential area of expertise.

That expertise may be your job. Most people who have worked for a company for a while have a decent understanding of the strengths and weaknesses of their organisation – and just as importantly have views about the competition they face, and the industry as a whole. You may have an interest in technology, fashion, sustainable living or alternative therapy. Whatever floats your particular boat there's a good chance that there's a company that is listed on the stock exchange that fits the bill.

On the radio show I always encourage people to try their hand at investing in a company on the stock exchange. Not only is it a lot of fun, but it also gives you a deeper level of understanding about how business works, and the role of the wider economy. Sure, you can read about stuff from a textbook, but it's not until you try your hand yourself that you really start to learn.

Let someone else do the hard work for you

Plan your work, work your plan ...

While I'm a fan of people taking the plunge and doing a bit of DIY investing, it's certainly not the focus of this book.

Investing is an option when you've eliminated personal debt, started saving 10 per cent of your earnings and can begin investing it in quality shares via a managed fund, then letting the magic of compound interest run its course over the space of your lifetime.

Sound boring?

In a world full of broken promises, this strategy is the cornerstone of investment and has made people extremely wealthy over time.

I like to think of myself as a Good Samaritan. In the past I've been known to help little old ladies across the road, I've donated money to charity, hell I've even bought a Kylie Minogue CD. My choice to invest for the long term has no altruistic motives, it's driven by pure unadulterated selfishness.

Learning about the magic of compound interest changed my way of thinking.

For the first time I realised that I could tread my own path regardless of what occupation I chose to do for the next fifty years. All that mattered was that I be smart with the money that I earn when I'm young and allow the time-honoured formula of interest and time to make me wealthy.

Many people mistake a high income for wealth. It's not true. As a stockbroker I've met people who earn hundreds of thousands of pounds a year and yet still have four fifths of sweet FA to their name. I also know people who despite never earning above the average

Get rich slow

This book has been designed to give you an overall strategy that can be implemented by anyone. There are a million different interpretations of how to best invest, but only a few have stood the test of time, which is why we have concentrated our search. So if you're hoping that I'm going to be covering short-term trading, options, futures, ostriches, gold or foreign exchange I'm going to disappoint you.

Investing involves purchasing assets and gaining the benefits associated with holding them over the long term. The golden rules of wealth haven't changed in hundreds of years, but you'd be surprised how many people try to bend them in the hope of getting rich quick. There are ways to become fabulously wealthy, but apart from winning the lottery, drug dealing and pornography, they never come quick.

If your parents had invested £10 000 in the stock market in 1973 it would be worth roughly £350 000 today. Key question: Why aren't they rich? I guess one answer could be that having children isn't cheap!

wage, have millions of dollars at their disposal. Reminds me of the old line – 'you don't have to be wealthy to invest, but you do have to invest to be wealthy'.

Mojo magic

There are three main reasons to invest in managed funds:

- Because there are more important things to do than worry about investing.
- The ability to diversify, so you spread your risk.
- They require a small initial investment and provide you with the opportunity to invest money regularly, on a monthly basis, for example.

1. Take the worry out of investing

In order to start investing it is advisable that you undertake a securities analysis course, spend every Saturday poring over company annual reports, and you're also required to devote at least two hours a week to financial porn of some description – business sections of the newspaper, investing magazines, business magazines ... not!

We all know what the oldest profession is. Possibly the second oldest is money management. Those of you who aren't interested in investing but still want to make sure your money is working hard can get a professional to do the leg work for you, by way of a managed fund. It sounds simple enough until you realise that there are hundreds of funds to choose from. If you have a penchant for investing in celluloid (as in movies, as opposed to cellulite, which is fat), racehorses, maybe a forest, local shares, foreign shares, stamps ... in fact anything, for practically anything you could possibly imagine investing in, there's bound to be a fund to do the investing for you.

Good fund managers are worth their weight in gold, with the emphasis on 'good' fund managers, as opposed to *ordinary* fund managers, and their close cousins *useless* fund managers.

While you lap up a latte, cruise the beach for talent or do some window-shopping, fund managers are going about the business of managing your money. They press the flesh with companies they're looking at investing in, spend hours delving into balance sheets and historical fundamentals, and devote a good part of their day researching companies to invest in.

2. Different places different faces

One of the cornerstones of investing is to be diversified. Diversification means not putting all your eggs in the one basket. Let's break it down with an example.

Each of us, without putting a complicated label on it, naturally diversifies – let's take your friends as an example. Most people have a 'diversified' group of friends. You have friends, don't you? How did you come about them? Most people don't hang around exclusively

Emotional Investment

Money evokes some powerful emotions. People have been known to make stupid decisions in the heat of the moment at casinos, like putting a week's wages on black because it hasn't come up for four spins. Invariably people lose a lot of money at casinos (that's why they can afford to pay the power bill for all those pretty lights). It's not just in the confines of casinos that people get caught up in the excitement of greed and fear, there are thousands of books on developing the right mind-set for investing.

It's human nature to pat yourself on the back when your investments are going up, but not be so happy when an investment takes a dive. As a stockbroker I've seen it happen time and time again-a client buys a stock at £4, it drops to £2, but the investor is holding onto it, believing (hoping) it will get back to what they paid for it. As old timers in the market will tell you-a stock doesn't know you bought it at £4! One of the advantages of having a fundo manager invest on your behalf is that it takes the emotion out of the investment decisions.

with the people they met at a scout camp when they were thirteen. Life presents us with different situations, experiences and surroundings, and along the way we click with different people and forge friendships.

You've probably got some crazy friends that are great to party with, share a laugh with and with whom you generally have a whale of a time.

No doubt you have friends that are there for you when you're studying, you know the *studious* types who, come exam time, you can knock on their door and say 'hey could you teach me that last ten weeks' physics ... this weekend?'

You have also probably got close friends in whom you confide, and who you can count on to cheer you up in times of need. Then there's your best friend – someone who has known you for lots of years, who you implicitly trust and who knows you better than anyone else.

Most of us have different relationships to fulfil different needs, and each serves a purpose. This, in essence, is what diversification is.

The same goes with our investments. On the Barefoot Investor radio show we have talkback where people call up and get investment advice. Invariably I get a call like this:

Me: Next up we have Morris on the line, he wants to talk about EasyJet. Go ahead Morris ...

Morris: Hi, I'm thinking about investing in EasyJet, you know because Stelios is an absolute gun, and the EasyJet stewardesses are like, totally hot, and they have cheap fares ...

Me: I'm a big fan of EasyJet, when I travel overseas I prefer to fly than take a dingy, and yes, you're right, the EasyJet stewardesses are great talent.

Morris Cool. So I'm good to go?

Me: Of course, oil prices go up which makes fuel for the planes more expensive, there's a lot of competition in the industry and global terrorism can all but kill tourism ...

Morris: So I'm not good to go?

Me: Hey, give it a go, because it's only a small holding in your big diversified portfolio. If EasyJet tanks, hopefully at least some of your investments will go up, levelling out your returns.

Morris: Ummm, I don't have any investments. I was just going to put all my money into EasyJet because I think it'll go up.

Me: What happens if it doesn't Morris?

Morris: That would be like, so not cool.

Me: I agree.

Morris: So I should invest in more than one company? Maybe add another that isn't so dependent on travel, like retailer Tesco? Perhaps a bank as well, they always do well ...

Me: It's a smart strategy Morris. Don't forget that we're just a little island in a big world. What if our economy tanks? You might want to invest in companies overseas that may not be as affected by a downturn in the UK.

Morris: But I only have a grand! I don't even have enough money to invest in five different companies operating in different industries, let alone investing overseas.

Me: For a grand you can invest in a managed fund where you pool your cash with other investors and gain access to hundreds of companies across the UK and the rest of the world.

Morris: I still like EasyJet.

Me: We all like them Morris, just make sure your focus is on your cash, not the stewardesses, when you put your money on the line.

3. Little by little

Fund managers like money – so much so that most funds will allow you to start investing with as little as £500 upfront. At the time of your initial investment you can also nominate the fund to directly debit your Mojo account each month and take your 10 per cent and invest it in the fund. In most funds the regular savings plan starts at about £50 a month.

This is what makes the Barefoot Plan so powerful – it requires no more thought than watching an episode of *CSI* – it's lock, load and forget. After sticking to this plan for a year you'll be amazed at just how much money you'll have. The best thing? Just like our compounding story of Sarah and Linda, it'll grow into a powerful force that allows you to do the things that are important to you.

How it works

Let's say you're on £450 a week, which equates to £1800 a month. Ten per cent of £1800 is £180, which is the amount that you will be directly debiting to your Mojo account. You've selected a good managed fund and signed up for their direct debiting monthly savings plan, which you contribute £180 to buy as many units in the fund as you can with your money.

Month	Unit Price	Number of units purchased
January	2.00	90
February	2.20	81
March	1.80	100
April	1.50	120
May	2.00	90
June	2.30	78

Let's take a look at your progress. In April when the price bottomed out to £1.50 you purchased 120 units, and in June when the price hit a high your £180 bought you just 78 units. Without looking at charts, subscribing to an investment newsletter, or trawling through economic historical analysis, you've managed to buy more units when the price is at its lowest and less as it nears its highs. Considering very few professional traders ever correctly pick the highs and the lows, you my friend are a bloody legend!

I know what you're thinking – sounds good Barefoot, but it's not like I'm going to go and purchase fifty shares here, thirty shares there ... the brokerage will kill me! Ah, but you overlook one important thing – the Barefooter doesn't fall for these traps. Paying yourself first, investing in growth assets over the long term, and this pound cost averaging technique are the centrepieces of the Barefoot Plan. Most managed funds have a savings plan that allows you to nominate to direct debit a certain amount each month into the fund.

Choosing a fund—outsourcing investments

My 'special situations' debacle taught me that past performance is not a guarantee of future results, which is simple logic. It's just that when we apply it to anything financial most of our brains melt to mush.

Classic example. Whitney Houston is one of the all time best-selling singers of the 80s with a string of monster hits, a multi-million dollar record deal and her face plastered all over magazines. Sitting there in the early nineties would you have been tempted to invest in her? How about Mariah Carey? Her album 'Music Box' was an all-time bestseller. I bet her prospectus was looking pretty good after that album. As we know both artists went through a considerable, shall we say, downtime, where they both still spent a lot of time in the gossip pages, but this time for all the wrong reasons: drug abuse, failed relationships, and the movies The Bodyguard and Glitter – say no more.

Managed funds

Managed funds aren't a particularly tricky thing to grasp. You pool your money with lots of other investors and let a professional do the hard slog for you. In the beginning the manager will issue each investor with units in the fund. If investors have collectively given the fund manager £10 million to invest, the fund manager will issue ten million 'units' with each unit equal to £1, for example. So, if you invest £1000, how many units would you get?

Um, one thousand? Touché old boy!

When the manager starts investing the ten million, the value of the overall portfolio may rise, fall or stay the same, but every day (or in some cases once a week) the fund manager gets the value (Net Asset Value) of all the investments she's put money into and then divides it by the out standing ten million units.

If the original £10 million is now worth £20 million each unit will be worth £2 (£20 million/10 million units). If the manager invests in a Kevin Costner epic and turns the initial £10 million into £5 million, the units will be worth 50 pence (£5 million/10 million units).

This is just an example – much like when you were at school and were made to watch those awful videos on the dangers of drinking too much alcohol. Sure there've been times when we've all hugged the porcelain express, but it doesn't happen every time. In much the same way, your managed fund's units won't usually double (or halve) in value over a short period – if it does, check you don't have Jessica Simpson as your fund manager.

Hunting for a fund

There's no need to hyperventilate at the thought of choosing your own fund. Most discount brokers have search engines that help you shortlist potential funds based on the criteria you set. In addition there are research houses that specialise in rating funds. The rating system is a bit like the way movies are rated. Keep in mind that *Titanic* was awarded five stars by one cinema buff. Fund ratings can be helpful but they are not always 100 per cent reliable.

The things to keep in mind when searching for a fund are:

1. The track record of the manager (over as many years as possible).
2. The fees the fund manager charges.
3. The asset class the fund invests in – for long-term mojo investing we want an equity (cool name for share) fund. Bonus points for a fund that has a portion of its investments overseas. After all, the UK stock market is only about a quarter the size of the US and there are many other interesting countries to invest in too.
4. Whether the company has a regular saving plan (and the minimum monthly requirement).
5. Ratings that research houses assign to various funds (but don't rely too heavily on this).

You don't have to sell your soul to make money

Excuse me Mr I'm a mister too, and you're givin' Mr a bad name Mr like you
BEN HARPER

Read the paper on any given day and you'd be hard pressed to find a company that isn't embroiled in some sort of controversy – huge oil conglomerates dumping oil at sea, mining companies polluting the water supplies of remote villages, pharmaceutical companies torturing animals under the guise of 'scientific research', multinationals setting up sweatshops in the Third World and so on.

Let's face the facts. There are companies that have done, and will continue to do, harmful and unethical things in order to pad the bank accounts of their shareholders. It's no surprise that these companies are rarely out of the headlines for their 'dirty deeds'.

I don't invest in them.

These companies are giving investing a bad name. If you've read this far, you'll quickly realise that I'm not your typical capitalist who chases a dollar regardless of how it's earned. I believe that investing in companies that do harm is a poor investment all round – they may earn money by doing damage, but sooner or later karma comes back and bites them (and their share price) in the bum. Take a look at the cigarette companies that now have to pay out billions of dollars in compensation.

I once spoke to a fellow stockbroker who's been in the business longer than I've been alive. He told me that when he started in the market no-one cared too much for ethical investing. The majority of the players in the market at that time were large-scale institutions and financial conglomerates – very few individuals invested personally. Consequently investing in companies that did the right thing never really hit the radar – the end game was producing a high return.

I want to work for a company that contributes to, and is part of the community. I want something not just to invest in. I want something to believe in.
ANITA RODDICK

I recently had the founder of the Body Shop, Anita Roddick, on Barefoot Radio. Anita is passionate about ethical investing, and is part of a movement she hopes will stop the exploitation of everything in the pursuit of profits.

Change is definitely in the wind. According to the Office for National Statistics around a quarter of British households now own shares directly and their holdings are, in total, worth around £200 billion. But many more of us own shares indirectly through pension funds or units trusts. As investing moves into the mainstream, more and more people are focusing on the business practices of the companies they invest in. Companies that are at the forefront of inno-vation and sustainable technologies, curing disease and promoting the wellbeing of all of us may well be some of the best investments you could ever make. Today being good in business makes good business sense.

When choosing a managed fund to invest in you can opt for an 'ethical' (also known as socially responsible) fund. But just what is an ethical fund manager? Visions of guys with dreadlocks playing hacky-sack in their offices and investing your money in high-quality weed couldn't be further from the truth. Most ethical managers have a two-stage process of determining whether a company is fit to be included in their portfolio.

The first is a negative screen, where ethical managers will screen out companies because their products or services are not desirable on ethical grounds. Often these will be detailed in the company's prospectus. Industries to be avoided might be alcohol and tobacco manufacturers, uranium miners, and gambling. Some fund managers take the process further and then do a positive screen where they look to include companies that are deemed to be desirable on ethical grounds.

One of our favourite Barefoot guests is UK-based Peter Hall, head of Hunter Hall Investment Management and currently Australia's biggest ethical fund manager. Peter says the old argument that in order to get good returns you have to 'sell your soul' and invest in companies that trade in sin is ludicrous. He should know, his flagship fund the Global Ethical Trust has achieved returns that have trounced the broader market and delivered consistent returns that are the envy of fund managers worldwide.

Nuts and bolts

There are three places to purchase a fund: fund supermarkets, Independent Financial Advisers (IFAs) and directly from the fund manager.

Shopping for funds is just like hunting down a good bargain – depending on where you go you'll pay more or less for what is essentially the same item. Let's look at how the game is played so you are better informed on how to get the best deal for you.

Wheeling and dealing

A typical fund manages hundreds of millions of pounds, all of it from ordinary people like you and me.

In Technical Talk 101, IFAs are the funds management industry's *network*. Traditionally people have gone to IFAs whose job it is to recommend different funds for their clients, and therefore the bulls of the money is directed to the funds by IFAS.

Herein lies the chicken and egg situation: fund managers don't invest money for people just to be fine upstanding citizens – they charge a percentage fee based on the amount of assets they manage. IFAs give them their clients' money to invest and earn money from the fees they charge.

IFAs want a slice of the action – not that there's anything wrong with that. A good IFA will give you advice tailored to your specific financial situation and recommend a fund that suits you. They also realise that because they are directing their clients' money to a fund manager who will be paid a fee, they should be paid for finding them the business.

Most managed funds charge three types of fees: entry and exit fees, and ongoing fees sometimes expressed as a Total Expense Ratio (TER). Just like banks, the managed funds industry has come up with a bewildering array of fees and charges, which make the process of comparing funds difficult.

Entry and exit fees

These are charged when you enter a fund and can range from zero up to 5 per cent of whatever you put in. If you put a £1000 into a fund with a 5 per cent entry fee, you're effectively only investing £950.

Exit fees work much the same, as you 'exit' the fund you can be charged a percentage fee as you were when you entered. Often fund managers will adopt a sliding scale for exit fees – the longer you leave your money in the fund the lower the fee, a way of encouraging investors to leave their money parked in the fund for a number of years.

Who gets your fees? You'd think that entry and exit fees would go to the stressed-out, sleep-deprived fund manager – alas, the money generated from your fees will usually be sent to the financial planner who put you into the fund.

OK, I know what you're thinking – why can't you cut out the middleman and go directly to the fund manager, thereby cutting out the hefty entry and exit fees? You can, but in most cases you'll still be charged an entry and exit fee regardless – it's just the fund managers way of looking after their network of financial planners.

In the dark old days when Bros wanted to know *'When will I, will I be famous?'* there was little choice – you were lumped with these fees whether you liked it or not. Thankfully these days discount brokers have emerged who will charge a fee for their service but will rebate most (if not all) of the entry fee in extra units in the fund. The good thing about these guys is that they have nifty search tools that you can use to search out the best fund for you.

Ongoing fees

Fund managers have expenses – golf club memberships, expensive lunches, Armani suits, repayments on their Mercedes, but that's another story. When you invest in a fund there are fees you must pay in return for having a professional manage your money. The fees are spent on compensation for the fund manager's staff, printing prospectuses, advertising, administrative costs, and commissions paid to the third party who you went through to get into the fund. These expenses are bundled up and expressed in the form of a Total Expense Ratio (TER), which is charged as a percentage of assets much like entry and exit fees. The table below charts the sorts of TER fees you will be charged.

TER and Other Fund Charges by fund type

	Typical TER range*		Typical %	
			Initial	Annual
Category	Low	High	Charge	Charge
UK Tracker Funds	0.35	1.0	0.0	0.1**
UK Corporate Bond	0.8	1.2	4.0	1.0
UK Government Bonds	0.8	1.2	4.0	1.0
UK Smaller Companies	1.2	1.6	4.0	1.5

UK Equity Income	0.9	1.6	5.0	1.5
Global Emerging Markets	1.4	2.2	5.0	1.5
North America (incl. Trackers)	0.8	1.6	5.0	1.5
North America Smaller Cos.	1.6	1.85	5.0	1.5
Europe ex-UK	0.7	1.6	5.0	1.5
European Smaller Companies	1.5	2.0	5.0	1.5

* Top 25 funds ignoring those claiming TER of zero
** Fund with lowest charges (Fidelity Moneybuilder UK Index)
Source: Investment Management Association

Smoke and mirrors

Most UK fund management groups have fairly transparent fee structures. Often the TER of the fund will be reflected in an annual charge that any investor in the fund will pay. In many cases you will be able to shave a big chunk off the fees by buying through a fund supermarket like Interactive Investor or Fidelity Fundsnetwork. Websites like this offer search tools that allow you to pinpoint the type of fund you might want to invest in, view the charges, and then buy or sell.

Remember though that some funds, like hedge funds, may have performance fees (where the fund manager gets a bonus for beating a benchmark like the all ordinaries), others may have a buy/sell spread which involves the fund manager incurring the expense of buying and selling units in the fund as people come and go. As a way of paying for this the fund manager may adjust the buy/sell spread so the costs aren't borne by long-term investors – but not always.

The only way to be sure of the fees you're paying is to read the offer document (called a prospectus) before you enter the fund. The prospectus will detail all the fees that you'll incur. The fund manager or fund supermarket must also provide you with a 'Key facts' document that will summarise all of the salient facts and figures about the fund, before you invest. Bear in mind that just because a fund has high fees doesn't mean that it has a greater likelihood of outperforming a fund that charges less.

Value of £20 000 invested for 20 years in two hypothetical funds each returning 8 per cent pa.

	FUND A TER 1.75%	FUND B TER 0.75%
Initial Investment	£20 000	£20 000
5 years	£27 082	£28 380
10 years	£36 671	£40 272
15 years	£49 655	£57 146
20 years	£67 237	£81 092
Difference		£13 855

Source: Vanguard

Prospecting with a prospectus

It shouldn't take too long using the search tools on most online discount brokers' websites to condense a short list of funds worthy of further investigation based on the criteria you've set. Armed with your list it's time to have a deeper look at the fine print. We do this by looking at the prospectus.

My 'special situations' debacle could have been avoided if I'd taken the time to read the prospectus. The prospectus is essentially an offering document, and is regulated by the corporate fuzz, the Financial Services Authority and Investments Commission.

Prospectuses are every eco-warrior's nightmare – they consume huge amounts of paper and few people read them thoroughly, principally because they're a bit *War and Peace* in volume. But, like Tolstoy, they can be rewarding. I would encourage everyone to read these documents – after all they set out the fees you will be charged, where your money will be invested, and what returns the fund manager is hoping to achieve over a set period.

Finally, after you've narrowed down your search to a few managers, don't underestimate your gut feeling when it comes to choosing a fund. The Barefoot Investor radio show interviews lots of fund managers, and the best are those that tell it like it is. Investing is largely commonsense: find a manager that speaks your language, and with whom you feel comfortable.

The best prospectuses are those that attempt to educate the potential investor about solid financial principles – not totally bamboozle them with complicated formulas and impressive sounding words.

After you've found the fund that's right for you, the prospectus will have a form for you to fill out. Attach a cheque to purchase units in the fund, supply details of your regular savings program and have the money directly debited from your Mojo account.

How do I find out how my fund is going?

You will receive regular statements from your manager, but if you can't wait that long, many fund managers have websites and investor phone lines, both of which allow you to check unit prices (usually updated daily).

You can also check out your fund's performance in the managed funds tables that are generally published weekly in major newspapers.

Index funds

Every night the TV newsreader says 'and in finance news, the FTSE 100 Index (known by everyone as 'footsie') closed lower/higher/flat today ... ' You'd be surprised how many 'informed' news watchers have absolutely no idea what the footsie is. The footsie is an index that tracks the overall movement of the share market by grouping together the largest companies and tracking their movement.

You can actually purchase very cheaply a fund that has the 100 shares that constitute the footsie. These are called index funds and they don't just track the footsie. There are plenty of indexes such as Standard and Poor's 500 or the Dow Jones, as well as overseas indexes that you can gain an exposure to by investing in a local index.

Why are they cheap?

Index funds have low fees because they don't employ highly paid fund managers to pick shares. All they do is they invest in whatever makes up the footsie – not too much leg work involved in doing that.

Why would you want to do that?

There have been studies here and overseas that tend to suggest that many active fund managers fail to beat 'the market' indexes (especially when you strip away all the fees they charge). Sometimes fund managers make mistakes and lose money, whereas if you're investing in the market, you're always going to get the market return – which is the benchmark that most stock pickers use to see how well they've done.

Finally, they give fantastic diversification. As little as £250 will give you a very small holding in every one of those 100 companies that constitute the footsie.

What happens if the stock market crashes?

Everyone knows that stock markets occasionally crash. Panic sets in and investors (or should I say gamblers) see stock prices going down and sell out, hoping to avoid the pain. Of course when the market is plunging everyone's got the same idea and therefore there are more sellers than buyers.

The media love a story, especially a dramatic one like a stock market crash where people 'lose' lots of money. Newspapers run front-page headlines like 'CRASH' and 'SHARE MARKET IN FREE FALL'. Television news bulletins run scenes of traders looking like they just had a date with Roseanne, self-proclaimed gurus come out of the woodwork saying the world will never be the same again – and everyone panics.

The average dude and babe on the street watch all this unfold and make the incorrect assumption that 'the share market is risky' – and that pisses me off big time.

The fact is that most of the headline hyperbole that you read and hear surrounding a stock market crash is written by journalists who are usually about as qualified to write on finance as the crew from *Queer Eye for the Straight Guy* are to do a makeover for a struggling Eritrean farm worker after a crop failure.

The media is there to sell newspapers, or garner television ratings, not in the role of financial adviser. If you let your financial decisions be based on what the media reports you're never going to be independently wealthy.

Boxing Day

I love Boxing Day. I've usually been way overfed by my mum and there's still plenty of leftovers to munch on. It's a public holiday, and the only thing on my agenda is to kick back with a beer in hand and watch the Boxing Day footie on TV.

My mother enjoys Boxing Day as well, but because of a different sport – shopping. Each Boxing Day the major retailers hold sales where they slash the prices of merchandise that hasn't sold in the Christmas rush. The big retailers make a fortune, based solely on the fact that there are so many people purchasing the 'bargains'.

Are there any similarities to a Boxing Day sale and a stock market crash? You betcha. Prices are falling and the media is commenting on the madness ... everybody is excited about the chance of picking up a bargain.

The difference of course is that when the stock market crashes people shit themselves, mainly because of that word – crash. What about when retailers advertise that prices are *crashing?* It's people's perceptions that make the difference. Because most people follow the herd, they never get truly wealthy.

Perspective

Throughout history after each 'crash' the stock market has *never failed* to go on to reach new highs. Sometimes it has taken a couple of months to surpass the previous high and sometimes it has taken years, but it always has.

Let's take a look at 1987, when 'I Should Be So Lucky' rocked the charts, *The Last Emperor* was the top movie and we discovered hair gel and shoulder pads. On October 19, the stock market crashed. Headlines like 'Panic sell-off grips New York' were common. Gurus came out of the woodwork and made acute observations like, 'The share market'so freefall is reaching the stage where it is feeding upon itself'. News pictures showed frantic brokers dumping stock.

People saw the value of their investments fall by 30 per cent or more in one week. They rang talkback radio crying foul, 'I've just lost thirty grand on the stock market!' – what they forgot to mention was that in the previous few years they'd nearly tripled their money.

Nonetheless, people were fearful, and were once again talking about how the stock market was 'risky'. Many sold their shares, fearing they would lose more.

But suppose you had been using the pound cost averaging strategy of putting a set amount of money into an investment each month. Your regular payment would have bought you fewer shares when the market was at its peals in early October 1987, but by the following month you were effectively at a Boxing Day sale – your fixed amount would have purchased you a heap of shares. Next, take a look at what happened to the market after the 'crash to end all crashes'. Did it make sense to do some bargain investing after the '87 crash? You betcha!

Pound cost averaging makes good sense in theory: the market crashes from time to time but always goes on to create new highs. All well and good, you say, but that doesn't stop you getting nervous when you go to put down *real* money – your money. No-one knows what the stock market will do tomorrow, next year, or ten years from now, but we can use history as a guide, and this tells us that over the long term share markets continue to rise.

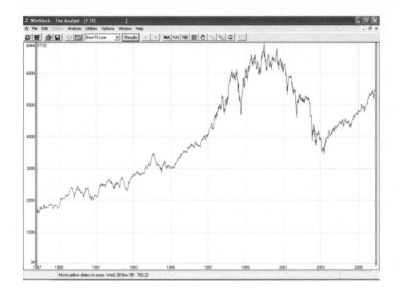

Beating the crashing blues

Big Brother was a phenomenon right across the world as one of the very first reality television shows to take off in a big way. The producers no doubt had a tough assignment convincing television executives to take a punt on a show that strayed away from the winning sitcoms that had been so successful since television had started. You can almost hear them, 'you mean you want to put a group of normal everyday people in a house and film them twenty-four hours a day, and then vote them off one by one? That's the basis for the whole show?'

I'm not ashamed to admit that the first series of *Big Brother* sucked me in big time. From an investment context if you had invested in the original *Big Brother* series, you would have done extremely well.

Then what happened? Each network saw an opportunity and got in on the game – suddenly we had *Celebrity Love Island, The Apprentice, Joe Millionaire, Wife Swap* and countless other reality television shows and suddenly reality television was on the nose.

There is an old investment saying that goes 'buy in gloom, sell in boom'. Financial markets, for all their high-speed-cable number crunching, technical charts and complex economic forecasting, still tend to get it wrong a lot of the time. Why? Richard FitzHerbert in his book *Blueprint for Investment* says that basically, the stock market is driven by greed and fear. We need to let go of those destructive motives and adopt a different approach. You can't do better than to follow the simple logic: buy when people are selling, and then sell when people are buying. Practically every investor on the face of the planet knows this but very few ever do it.

The number one question I get as a stockbroker is: Is the market high right now?

The exchange usually goes something like this:

Me: If you're wearing blue underpants today it's a good time to buy.

Client: What the hell are you on about? What have my underpants got to do with whether it's a good time to buy or sell you weirdo-pinko-sicko? I want to know if you think the market's going up, in which case I'll buy, or if you think it's going down I'll sell. In any case, I think you're a deviant, and I want another stockbroker.

The fact is that no-one can consistently pick when the market is going to go up, down, or sideways. In *Winning the Loser's Game* author Charles D. Ellis says, 'Market timing is a wicked idea. Don't try it – ever.'

Is it all about blue underpants?

Maybe! Actually no, that was a joke.

Herein lies the problem: you can make a lot of money by buying low and (eventually) selling high, but the experts agree that as no-one has a crystal ball, it's practically impossible to pinpoint when the best time invest is.

If you follow the program outlined in this book you *will* effectively time the market almost to perfection, without the use of tarot cards or Bruce Willis's sixth sense. How? By using the well-known, time-honoured strategy of pound cost averaging. With PCA on your side we'll soon have you timing the market and beating the pants off the so-called experts.

Part of the beautiful simplicity of the Barefoot Investor plan is that you take the 10 per cent you directly deposit into your Mojo account and pop it straight into a managed fund that has a monthly savings plan.

Crystal ball gazing

I don't have a crystal ball. I can't tell you what the next hot sector is going to be – and neither can anyone else. Yet, over the long term, there are factors we can foresee that will have a major impact on the world in which we live.

The emergence of China

Over the next thirty years China's move from communism to capitalism will create economic growth in Australia, and the entire world, as it opens itself up to new markets. China represents about 20 per cent of the world's population. That's 1.3 billion people becoming wealthy enough to consider purchasing the goods that are available in the West: cars, furniture, clothes, shoes – practically everything we take for granted in the Western world. Companies throughout the world will need to raise their output to accommodate the needs of a couple of billion new customers! Sounds pretty good doesn't it? I haven't even factored the billion or so Indians that will soon become an economic force!

There are other factors on the horizon for us as investors – globalisation and technological advancement.

Globalisation

Some people like the concept of a global village with limited trade barriers and others don't. I'm sure each of us has a view of some sort. Mine is that it's bigger than all of us, and it's a revolution that is taking place as we speak, fuelled by technological breakthroughs and the opportunities the new world order gives poorer countries to rebuild their economies to exploit markets as they open up.

The world is an amazing place. Sure there is war, famine, drought and poverty, yet we are living in exciting times. There will be fortunes made over our lifetime, and the only way to get a piece of it is to become a part-owner of some of the best companies in the world.

The Mojo action plan

Following the principles of Barefoot Bondage you will be depositing a percentage of your wage via direct debit into an online high interest account known as your Mojo Money Account. When this account has £1000, which depending on the amount you're debiting could take a couple of months or the space of a year, it's time to start looking at investing each new contribution. Paying yourself first is one of the most important things you'll ever do for yourself. It'll ensure that as time passes your money grows faster than you can work for it.

5

Have a Backup Plan

BAREFOOT STEP 5

Congratulations! You've made it to the final Barefoot step, your backup plan.

This ensures that now you've done all the hard work, no-one can take your new-found (and building) wealth from you.

In the final step of the Barefoot Plan we cover:
- How one incident can ruin everything you've achieved – and anything you do in the future, and how to make sure it never happens to you.
- What insurance you need and what you don't.

- How to cover yourself, without spending an arm and a leg.
- Everything you ever wanted to know about super-annuation but were too afraid to ask.
- How to prevent money from screwing up your relationships.
- The shoebox filing system that ensures you get a new pair of shoes each year *and* keep up-to-date records!

Always use protection

Insurance may not be on the top of your list of things to research. For many of us it comes well below grooming tips like 'washing my hair'. A few years ago I learnt my lesson the hard way.

Turning eighteen was special for me. It wasn't just the ability to (legally) drink alcohol, but that other prize of adulthood – a driver's licence.

Not content with a safe, reliable first car like most of my mates, my vehicle of choice was a 1966 XP Falcon, bought for A$500 from a farmer out the back block of Nowhere Ville. The car still drove – although twenty odd years of neglect sitting in a paddock meant it was in need of a lot of attention, not to mention its dodgy two tone job applied using house paint. In the great Aussie tradition of men bonding over metal, restoring the XP Falcon was going to be, in the words of my mother, 'a father and son project'.

The day I turned eighteen, I sat for my licence and got it. Back at the ranch, the father and son project was working about as well as a dentist without a drill – we'd done pretty much bugger all.

So there I was, eighteen, licence in hand, and a car still covered in house paint and in dire need of repair. Nevertheless, I was determined to take it for a spin, against my father's advice due to it being unregistered, unroadworthy and uninsured.

Itching to get behind the wheel I piled two of my best mates into the Falcon and set out for the highway to 'open 'er up'. There we were, three kids in a heap of junk that was in its prime before any of us were even a stirring in our old man's pants, hurtling down the highway at sixty miles an hour.

I now had my licence, but I'd never been let loose without a parent in the passenger seat or a driving instructor and here I was behind the wheel with two mates egging me on. Then the unthinkable happened. After years of retirement laying idle in a country paddock, the car wasn't happy being taken out on the open road and flogged to within an inch of its life. It stopped – engine failure. Being an inexperienced driver I panicked and slammed on the brakes. The HGV behind me hit the anchors, but not quickly enough. If we had been in a modern-day small car we would've been wrapped around the dashboard, but in 1966 cars were made from 100 per cent Aussie steel, which was our saving grace.

As I jumped out I was starting to sweat. I was eighteen – just a kid, and I was about to encounter an angry trucker. Almost as an afterthought, I realised I had no insurance and the car wasn't even registered! Luckily for me the trucker thought it was all quite funny. He took a quick look at his truck, which only had, in his words, 'a bit of bark off it' and was on his way.

That night I learnt a very valuable lesson about insurance from my parents. I had got off lucky. Sure, my father had a tear in his eye when he saw the damage done to the car, but that was nothing compared to what could have happened.

As my parents explained to me, if I had collected another car, or worse, if I had hit someone, I would have been financially ruined. I had worked so hard establishing my investment portfolio, one stupid act could have wiped it all out (and then some) in a split second.

Why have insurance?

Life is full of surprises. A branch of a tree blown down in a high wind? How about the chances of stepping under a bus tomorrow?

The fact is that even though people don't know what'll appear in the crystal ball from one moment to the next, most of us want to make sure we are taken care of, should things go a bit pear-shaped.

Three Panadol, a box of Bandaids and a condom don't exactly constitute an effective insurance policy.

Thinking about insurance is about as interesting as watching a Ben Affleck flick, so I'm going to break it down to the basics: why you need it, what you need, and how to avoid getting ripped off.

Think of insurance in terms of when you were at school and still living with your parents. You were living at home, and most of life's curve balls were insured by your parents. Need to go to the doctor? Sure, we'll pay for that. Tonsils need to come out? Here's some ice cream and we'll pick up the tab. Need braces? Cool, done, just don't kiss any girls, freak.

Was it free? Well, yes and no. For most parents to assume the risk, a large majority of them like to molly-coddle you, and dish out advice on the way you should live your life.

Bottom line – sometimes shit happens, no matter how cautious you are. When it does happen, without insurance you are risking total financial ruin. Think about all the hard work you're putting in getting your finances worked out – one chance occurrence could hit your dreams for six.

Now don't confuse me for a dodgy insurance salesman painting pictures of pain in order to fulfil my monthly quota. While insurance is an important safeguard in the event of disaster striking often it's easy to get carried away and end up with unnecessary cover. Remember the primary purpose of insurance is to ensure that when the shit hits the fan you are able to pull out your very own version of the get-out-of-jail-free card and let the big boys at the insurance company sort it out for you.

Important no matter what:
o Car insurance (if you've got a car).
o Health insurance (if you've got a body).
o Contents insurance (if you've got possessions).

Kinda important, but not essential:
o Life insurance.
o Disability insurance.
o Trauma insurance.

If there's no-one to look after besides yourself, whether you take out these last three policies will depend on your income. They may also be offered by your pension fund, so check with them first.

I'm not a big believer in young people getting much more than that mainly because – well we're young, (mostly) healthy, and probably don't have anyone else at this point in time relying on the income we earn.

Insurance explained simply

As we've discussed, insurance can be a mighty complicated beast, and I believe it's made that way to utterly confuse you so that you are tempted to spend more money than you need to. Here's how to sort out what it all means.

Throughout time people have been getting themselves into all sorts of trouble. You might have an accident, maybe that smoking habit finally gets the better of you or perhaps you perceive driving as a blood sport, whatever.

The whole deal is essentially this. Shit happens, and unless you've got mountains of cash set aside for the day it hits the fan you'd better pass on that risk to someone else, and that someone else is likely to be an insurance company.

Insurance companies perform a fairly basic transaction. They agree to shoulder a particular risk (such as a car accident), in exchange for a fee, which is known as a premium.

Insurance is essentially a numbers game. Insurance companies are excellent at working out the odds of people having car accidents, falling ill, or getting broken into, principally because they're in the business of mopping up the mess. Because it's their arse on the line, insurance companies like to assess the likelihood of the event being insured against occuring before you take out the particular policy.

If you're an extreme sport fanatic who smokes fifty ciggies a day and who regularly incites bar-room brawls, how willing would an insurance company be to insure your health? The numbers game says there's a lot better chance of you getting seriously injured than that of a health nut whose idea of living on the edge is going to an Elton John concert. To compensate for this high risk the insurance company will demand a higher fee.

The basic nuts and bolts of insurance are the same, be it car insurance, health insurance or contents insurance.

In return for the insurance, you will pay a set premium (which is just a fancy name for a bill) for the term of the cover. The amount you pay for the premium is determined by two factors:

- **The likelihood of the event happening, and whether you personally increase or decrease that risk.** A commonly cited example is male drivers under the age of twenty-five. Insurance companies know that statistically this group of drivers is more likely to be involved in accidents, hence their premiums are more expensive.

- **The other variable that will determine how much insurance costs you is the amount of risk that you're willing to assume yourself.** In the event of a claim you can choose to pay an initial amount towards your costs (known as an excess). In doing so, the insurance company will usually lower your premium, since it won't have to bother doing all the paperwork for a pissy little claim. Another advantage of this is that when you make a claim in most cases the insurance company will increase your premium for making that claim. So by shouldering some of the risk you are able to cut down on potentially higher premiums in the future, while simultaneously lowering the amount you have to pay each year.

Finally, there is the insurance policy. This tome of a document sets out the conditions of the insurance policy and the circumstances under which the insurance cover can be claimed. The problem with most insurance policies is that they tend to be largely indecipherable, and about as readable as an instruction manual. Even though this is the case, it is extremely important to read through the policy, or get an insurance agent to explain it to you (either verbally or written), so you can be sure just what you're covered for, and, just as importantly, what isn't covered.

Car insurance

Most people's first experience with insurance is insuring their car. If you were anything like me, in the first exhilarating highs of owning your own freedom machine, insurance was probably an afterthought.

There is a lot of confusion when it comes to car insurance. There are three main types – third party, third party fire and theft, and comprehensive.

Compulsory third party

Third party insurance is compulsory. It protects others and their property from accient that you might cause. If you have an accident

– and it's your fault – the insurer will cover any claims made by the third party, but it won't pay out any damage to you or your car. You have to be able to show that you have this cover when you tax your car.

In other words, the deal with compulsory third party is that it insures you (or anyone else that drives your car) against anyone who is injured in a car accident. People have been know to get pretty messed up in car accidents and the cost of hospitalisation and rehabilitation can run into hundreds of thousands of pounds.

Let's look at what type of car you drive and see what insurance is best for you.

My car gets me from A to B, sometimes even C ... third party fire and theft

This car isn't a bomb, but it never used the word 'luxury' as part of its initial marketing campaign. In short it's a nice reliable car that gets you around, which is a good thing because you rely on your car to get you to work and as a makeshift bedroom for you and your boyfriend. You couldn't imagine your life without your car.

Third party fire and theft cover could be the best insurance for you. This covers you for damages to other parties, and also gives you limited cover if your car is lost or damaged by fire or theft.

Obviously it's going to cost a little more than basic third party, but if you'd be lost without your car (due to fire or theft), this may well be a cost-effective alternative to comprehensive insurance, although it is very important to investigate the exclusions of different policies in relation to fire, theft, and loss of your vehicle.

I love my car ... comprehensive

Your car isn't simply a means of transportation; it's your pride and joy. You've been known to wake up in the middle of the night all hot and sweaty as you fantasise over the new monogrammed floor mats you've just bought. You've spent serious amounts of money acquiring (or modifying) this piece of steel.

Nine quick tips for car insurance

1. Make sure you have third party insurance as a minimum. Your car may not be worth much but the damage that it can do to others can be. It's financial suicide without it.

2. Don't modify your car. Don't be one of those people who have a night-club-like sound system in your car. For one, it makes your car more susceptible to theft which means your insurance costs will go up, and secondly you'll look (and sound) like a wanker. Also, it makes you a target for the cops.

3. Take a defensive driving course. You may be able to get a rebate from your insurer for taking the course, it may even teach you how to keep within the white lines – either way it's one of the best things you can do.

4. Think about your no-claim bonus. There's not much point in filing a claim for a small claim if it endangers your no-claim bonus, so make sure you do the sums before you file a claim.

5. After you turn 25, take another look at your car insurance – it may well become cheaper.

6. Garage your car where possible.

7. Always shop around and take the highest excess you can afford. Remember that you only insure yourself for things that would financially kill you, and you want to keep your insurance costs down. Choosing the highest excess you can afford will help achieve it.

8. Read your policy carefully – if you don't understand it, don't sign it. Get someone to explain the crux of the policy to you, bonus points for getting their thoughts in writing.

9. Drive carefully – not only will you save on insurance claims, but you get to live as well – what a deal!

If you want to make sure that your car is fixed regardless of whether an accident is your fault or not, or replaced if you misplace it, comprehensive insurance is probably your best option. Be warned however, that this is the most expensive form of car insurance, so it doesn't make a whole lot of sense to spend £2000 a year insuring a car that's only worth £3000.

Contents insurance

Contents insurance covers the value of your contents in the event of fire or theft. It's usually seen as something for the socks with sandals brigade – not for young people, and consequently few people who rent take out contents insurance.

Take a quick look around your house. OK, so it's not exactly the Taj Mahal, but think about having to replace *everything* if you get robbed or the whole thing goes up in flames. People tend to look at the big-ticket items like electrical and whitegoods, but what about your extensive CD collection? What about your jewellery, or clothes for that matter?

I've had mates that have been robbed blind and what I've learned from their experience is that even though the contents of their house didn't come straight from the Country Life guide to yuppie living, they had spent years accumulating stuff, and in one swift break and enter they were back to zero.

Recent statistics on burglaries in the UK show that in a recent 12 month period there were around 820 000 burglaries – around four for every thousand people. And there are around 55 000 house fires every year in the UK.

But let's not paint the worst possible scenario. Let's say you just get burgled, and they take the usual stuff. Buying a new computer, a new TV, DVD player, all at the one time, is probably something few people could do without racking up some huge credit card debt. This is why you need contents insurance, but only half of all renters have this insurance.

The good thing with this type of insurance is it's pretty cheap.

Contents insurance will generally cost you a couple of hundred pounds each year, and for that you will get a set pound amount of coverage for your goods, such as £10 000, £20 000, £30 000 or £50 000 for all you hot shots.

OK, so I've sold you on the benefits of home contents insurance, but what if you live in a shared house or flat? While its possible to find a policy that will cover all your housemates, insurance companies by and large don't offer a group policy to cover all

Eleven quick tips for contents insurance

1. Choose a reputable insurance company: There are different insurance companies that will offer you slightly cheaper deals on your insurance, but Barefoot Investors understand that the real reason that you bother with insurance is so that if the worst does happen, you want to be with an insurance company that has a reliable history of paying.

2. Create a list of everything you own before you start looking for insurance: When investigating contents insurance, you might find that the insurance company has a minimum amount of cover – say £5000. At face value, for most people five grand can sound like a hell of a lot of money but the fact is that you probably have a lot more than that, when thought of in terms of replacement value.

3. Shop around: Compare prices and the features of insurance policies before you buy so you can get competitively priced insurance, and importantly the cover that's right for you.

4. Always insure your contents with a reinstatement/replacement policy: Even though it costs a little more it's well worth it.

5. Get a clear understanding of how your insurance company defines 'replacement or reinstatement of goods': How do they work out what an equivalent standard for your goods is?

6. Read through your policy contract so that you know exactly what you're covered for: Companies that offer cheap insurance often have a lot of exclusions (stuff you're not covered for).

7. Insuring valuable items: Insurers usually cap household items at a certain amount. So if you have a family heirloom (other than your dad's Bobby Charlton football shirt) like jewellery or expensive artwork you may need to list each item separately and possibly pay an additional premium.

8. Use a camera or camcorder to film your valuables: If you have to make a claim, having all your valuables photographed should help to make sure it all goes as smoothly as possible and you aren't parking your bum on bare floorboards for too long.

9. The more documentation and evidence that you have to back up your claim the better: You can use a video camera to record all the goods as evidence, take photos, keep receipts for any of the goods you want to insure and get valuable items engraved.

10. Keep photocopies of all your insurance information and documentation somewhere other than your house: Here's the deal, you've been really good and kept great documentation of all the contents that you've insured. Unfortunately the house goes up in flames and so does all your evidence and documentation. It's commonsense but you'd be surprised how many people get caught out.

11. No porkies: You'll find in the small print that you have a duty of 'positive disclosure' to tell the insurance company anything that might increase the risk of you making a claim or of getting burgled. If your insurance company smells something fishy, and you're caught out, it can refuse to pay your claim. Insurers are experts in detecting inconsistencies, so if you think that you can pull the wool over their eyes, forget about it. Smarter people than you have tried to stretch the truth and have ended up counting the financial loss.

tenants. Therefore it's advisable to take out individual cover and insure what *you* own.

Let's go shopping.

When shopping for contents insurance, you'll probably find that most policies are roughly the same price. Therefore, your choice comes down to the insurer with the best reputation for paying up. See the eleven quick tips for contents insurance below for more information on this.

You'll also have to choose between an indemnity policy and a replacement/reinstatement policy. What the? The choice between these two types of policies rests on how the insurance company values your contents. An indemnity policy will tend to be cheaper than the reinstatement policies because your contents will be insured for their *market* value.

I'm not really a fan of this type of policy, and here's why. Let's say you've moved out of home and have taken your parents' old TV which still works a treat, but it's been around so long you all camped in front of it to watch Andy and Fergy's wedding.

If you get burgled, with a reinstatement policy you get a shock when you find that the insurance company may only give you a £25 cheque, which is the 'market value' for the old TV This really isn't cool, because it worked well and now with the new season of *Big Brother* coming up it's a must have. Except now you've got to put your hand in your pocket and fork out the rest for a new TV, which ultimately defeats the purpose of insurance – peace of mind. If you've got a lot of old stuff, or hand-me-downs, an indemnity policy is probably not really what you want, because unlike over-the-top retro furniture shops, insurance companies won't put a premium on your chocolate brown velour couch.

On the other hand reinstatement/replacement policies allow you to insure your goods for the cost of replacing them with new items of an equivalent standard, and although they are a little more expensive, it means that anything that's insured will be replaced. When you've been through the stress of getting robbed, the last thing you need is to worry how you're going to find the extra cash to replace all your stuff that the insurance company won't cover.

Health insurance

There's been a lot written about health insurance, and much of it is an aid for sleep deprivation. Access to quality healthcare is one of the major issues in the UK today. Hospitals aren't as cool as the gang on *ER* make out. Here's how to cover yourself.

Do you have a body? You might want to think about health insurance. Which is worse – crashing your car or crashing your body? Can you trade in your old body for a better-equipped, smoother, more fuel-efficient, or faster one? You might want to think about health insurance.

Because our largest generation, the Baby Boomers, is going into full grey-hair mode our already overstretched medical resources are being put to the test. As the costs keep rising you can bet that the issue of healthcare and who pays for it won't be slipping off the radar.

In the UK our healthcare system, known as the NHS, is basically free for all residents. But the rising cost of healthcare is taking its toll on the public purse, and despite what the government might say, the system is creaking at the seams. There are issues over hygiene in hospitals, waiting lists for operations, and if you are one of the fortunate ones with access to an NHS dentist – congratulations. Despite this, we still have some of the best medical facilities in the world and, if you live outside a major city, you have probably been pretty pleased with any treatment you've had.

So if you're already paying for it, and we've got some of the best facilities in the world, why bother with the extra cost of joining a health insurance plan?

Reality check to aisle one ...

Personally I'm a realist. I hope that I never have to go to hospital, but

I understand that at some unknown point in time I'll need to, and when I do I want to have access to the best facilities available, and to have them when I need them.

Even though I am responsible for recklessly damaging my body on many occasions, including the unnecessary obliteration of millions of brain cells in relation to drinking, trying to save a few bucks by scrimping on health insurance is a dumb decision.

Eight quick tips for health insurance

1. Consider using an insurance broker. Shopping for health insurance can be a nightmare! The services of a insurance broker are free and they can provide you with a number of alternatives that are tailored to your needs. Just make sure they disclose all their commissions so you are aware they could be pushing a particular product.

2. Focus on the hospital coverage. Try to get a policy that covers you for most operations in most hospitals. You never know what's going to strike you down, or where it'll be for that matter. The ancillary cover should be a secondary consideration.

3. Take the highest excess you can afford to lower the cost of the premium.

4. The waiting period. When you are joining a health fund remember that each scheme will have a waiting period before they'll start paying out on things. It's good to check what those waiting periods are.

5. Look at where you spend your money on ancillaries (extras that help you to look after yourself – homeopathy, chiropractor etc.) and choose a fund that offers quality coverage for the things that you regularly use.

6. Some funds offer a discount if you pay your premiums via direct debit. This can lower the cost of health insurance.

7. If you haven't joined a scheme by the time you are 30, have a think about it. Your premiums will be higher the older you get.

8. Read your policy carefully.

Pensions

I can't see myself with grey hair, or worse, no hair at all. I'm in my mid-20s and I'm never, ever growing old. It's just not fashionable. The alternative to not becoming old is dying, which is not really that cool either. The only upside is that I won't really need money then. All things considered, I'm not planning on being dead anytime soon, and as a result I will probably wake up in many years time looking at the world through Coke-bottle lenses and with a body that resembles Alfred Hitchcock, in which case I'll need money to cheer me up.

The reason we need pensions is that Brits are pretty poor savers by world standards. A recent survey by Sainsbury's Bank said that on average we had only £3000 in cash savings, 30 per cent has savings of less than £500 and that 12 per cent of us had no savings at all.

As the baby boomers retire en masse, golf clubs and retirement complexes are licking their lips, but the government certainly isn't. It can't afford to keep all the oldies in flat caps and corn plasters for the whole of their retirement and, just like the day before you get paid, there's simply not enough cash in the kitty to take care of the bill.

The reason for the problem is that we are all living longer. When your granddad retired it was a fair bet that most retirees would only live until just past their 70th birthday. Now our retirement funds have to support us for not just five or six years but until we are past our 80th birthday, and in some cases a long way past it.

While the state pension, which everyone in work contributes to through National Insurance contributions, can help, it simply isn't enough now for most retirees to fulfill the ambitions they might have in retirement. It hasn't really kept pace with the rising cost of living. Because of this the government is encouraging everyone to make their own additional pension provision, either through the company they work for, or by taking out a personal pension on their own account. Because of this, the contributions you make into a private pension scheme are fully allowable against tax.

Even this isn't enough for the government to balance the books, and the result is that the retirement age at we qualify for the state pension (60 for women and 65 for men) may have to be increased.

If you can't face the prospect of working until you are nearly 70, then it's up to you to build up your own nest egg so you can stick two fingers up the government and retire when you damn well want to.

Most of us with jobs that provide pensions probably resent the fact that 6 per cent of our salary goes into our pension scheme, even though the employer matches that contribution. But the fact is that most companies can't afford to provide us with a guaranteed pension (a so-called defined benefit scheme) where we might retire on two-thirds our finishing salary.

Most private employers have shut down schemes like this and now simply collect contributions and use them to amass a fund that, if you leave your job, you can take with you and invest in a private pension contract.

There are a couple of rules with pensions. One is that the earlier you start contributing to one, the bigger the fund you will have when it comes to retirement – thanks to the magic of compound interest.

The normal way of providing a retirement income is to use your fund to buy an annuity. This provides a guaranteed annual income from the date you retire to the day you die, after which the annuity provider keeps your capital. Annuities are based on life expectancy, so if you have £100 000 in your pension fund and want to retire at 60, it will buy you less annual income than if you retired at 65. Similarly, if you drink and smoke heavily, or have poor medical record, you will get a bigger income each year from your annuity, because the annuity provider is betting on you dying sooner.

A typically annuity rate for a reasonably healthy 65 year old is around 6.25 per cent. So if you want a retirement income of £25 000 you need to start off with a pension fund of £400 000.

It gets worse.

For example, the government is very tough on letting anyone dip into their pension fund early. And it also makes it compulsory for us to use our pension fund to buy an annuity if we reach age 75. That way it has fewer bag ladies to cope with.

Sacrificing your salary

I have sacrificed my salary on many occasions, mainly in the pursuit of female companionship. The government is pretty keen on you sacrificing some of your salary too, not in the name of getting some action, but into your pension fund – because it reduces the risk you'll need a handout from the government when you retire.

Needless to say it treats its own pretty well. Most government employees get pretty generous pensions, index-linked to boot.

Are pensions a good idea? Yes and no. Unless you are paying a lot of tax and you're pretty well heeled, sacrificing the money you earn today for some sort of future benefit doesn't really make financial sense. One problem is that governments are continually moving the goalposts on pensions, in other words you could be exposed to significant legislative risk.

Remember, though, that this is completely separate from setting up your Mojo account, controlling your spending, and accumulating savings and investments. Remember that a pension fund is really just a tax benefit combined with compulsory saving. Focus on what you think you need to retire on, have a look at what the state pension can provide and work out how you can manage to accumulate what you need to make the difference. Remember that getting there will take some persistent saving. Don't rely on winning the lottery to meet your objectives.

Gather all your pension funds together

If you're like me you will have had quite a few jobs over the years. In the UK, any job that pays a regular wage will probably have come with pension contributions attached. You probably forgot about them when you changed jobs. If you do nothing about them, they will simply accumulate quietly and you'll end up not knowing how much you have saved up and get a few quid a week from each one when you reach 65. It's better to have them all in one place and for about the last thirty years it's been comparatively easy to get hold of all your previous fund contributions.

A few years ago I decided to spend a couple of hours to track down all my different pension funds and roll them all over into one place. I reckoned that if I got them all together and cut down on the admin fees, I would be ahead of the game. Double that when you take into account the effect that compound interest can have on even the smallest balance over thirty years.

It was like compiling a list of all the people I'd snogged at parties. I took a trip down memory lane and wrote down all of the places I'd worked. Then I contacted my former employers and asked them if I could transfer my contributions into the pension I had with my current full-time job.

If you can't remember all of the places you've worked, it could be that Alzheimers has struck very early. Only joking! You can contact

Round up your pension

1. Ring your former employers and get the details of your contributions and how to transfer them out.

2. Contact the department of Work and Pensions about any loose ends. Check out their website for a wealth of pensions information (some of which you would rather not know about).

3. Round up you pension contributions by using the free online Pensions Tracing Service, available from The Pensions Service web site or get a form by phoning them on 0845 6002 537.

HM Revenue and Customs, which should have a record of all of the small holdings that have been administered in your name.

The price of love

Love and money: the two go hand in hand, especially in the sleazy neighbourhood where I live. It may seem strange that I have included a section dealing with the financial perils involved in relationships, but it's an issue that is far too quickly overlooked by couples in their desire to nest.

It's long been known that money problems always have been, and probably always will be, high on the list of relationship woes, and can be attributed to many break-ups (that and the whole monogamy thing).

We're different from our parents' generation, who by and large were married young and started pumping out kids fairly early on. Now, at the same age, their children's level of commitment is usually defined by using a Tesco Clubcard.

That being said, as a generation we are cohabiting longer and getting married later in life, and who could blame us? With university and the dreaded student loans, skyrocketing housing prices and a labour market that is fickle at best, the option of getting a house in the burbs and a BMW seem like a pipe dream.

Money comes and money goes, but broken hearts can last forever. By sitting down and talking openly about your finances you may avert a potential disaster down the track. When all is said and done money isn't as important as our relationships.

Joint accounts

Do you need a joint account so that you can both have access to funds for daily expenses? The issue of joint accounts can be a tricky one. There are some couples that I have met that want to share every-thing, and that by doing so it proves their love for the other person.

As much as I am a believer in the power of love, I still err on the other side of caution when it comes to sharing bank accounts, and underline that when sharing credit obligations.

Let's start with a joint bank account. This is an account that is set up in both partners' names and either may sign off on transactions, giving each partner equal access to funds.

There are advantages to sharing a joint bank account. For one the minimum balance requirement may be more easily met when there are two of you contributing cash. Another advantage is the 'you paid for dinner so I'll pay you back by buying that much of the groceries' hassle. A shared bank account can also be a good way to jointly save for a mutually agreed purchase such as a holiday, with each of you contributing to the pool of funds.

That being said there are advantages to keeping things singular. For starters, there's a lot to be said for a little independence when it comes to how you spend your cash. Unlike a joint bank account, where one partner can go through your transactions with a fine-tooth comb and question your every purchase, with a separate account your money remains your business. There's also the advantage that should things turn sour it's less of a headache if you have individual accounts.

Joint credit

The next decision that couples are likely to look at is avoiding STDs. No sexual health lectures from the Barefoot Investor, in this case STD stands for Sexually Transmitted Debt.

The phrase 'joint and severally liable' = your arse is on the line if things don't run smoothly. I'm not a big fan of couples getting into debt together, when a couple go into debt either through a credit card or a loan it opens both parties up to significant financial risk and unless you are very careful you may end up paying the lion's share of a debt if your partner gets into financial difficulty.

Another potential problem may involve your partner not having the same degree of tardiness that you do when it comes to paying their bills, which may result in both of you getting a black marks against your credit ratings. Remember that lenders don't really care if you have issues. All they want is their money to be repaid, and if you both have your names on the agreement they're not going to be too picky which one of you pays it, they just want it paid.

If the temptation is too much and you do decide to join forces and take the vow of credit, its always good to keep a written record as to who is paying what, and who will eventually be the owner of any goods bought. Again, without sounding too negative, the last thing you want when you're going through a break-up is the unnecessary squabbling over who owns what.

We need to talk

Often you'll know more about your partner's CD collection than you will about their finances, and if this is the case you'll need to dig a little deeper.

Sometimes people feel vain or materialistic when they talk about money with their partner, as if discussing it cheapens the relationship or the romance. A more pragmatic approach would be that the two of you are mature enough to discuss openly your financial affairs for the good of the relationship.

My view is that if you're willing to share toothbrushes, you should be willing to have an open and frank discussion about money at least once. As Oprah would put it, it helps you to get to know each other on a 'deeper level'.

If you're taking the step of moving in with someone you probably have a good idea of their spending habits, but it's always good to talk about whether your partner adheres to some kind of budget, and whether they are in the habit of living from pay cheque to pay cheque, or, if they prefer to have a surplus of funds for when the unexpected arises.

The answers to these questions will give you vital clues as to the financial make-up of your significant other.

Another important question to discuss with your partner is the (gasp!) amount of money they earn, and this time if it's a guy, get him to tell you straight, seeing as the last time he probably mentioned it was on the third date when he was really trying to impress. The amount you earn determines a whole range of things, most importantly your ability to pay bills.

The second thing to ask is if your partner has any borrowings, and how much they commit to paying off those borrowings, reason being if she misses a payment and they repossess her sofa it may not be much fun snuggling on the tile floor.

The third thing to talk about is their thoughts on gambling, and/or financial risk-taking. The girl who looks sweet and innocent could have a one-armed bandit addiction which means she's always hitting you up for cash come rent day, or your boyfriend may like to trade the market and in doing so take big risks.

Relationships are hard enough as it is without the unnecessary burden that money puts on them. Taking the time to discuss the issues outlined here is a great way of averting unnecessary heartache in the future.

Cohabitation and prenuptial agreements

Something old, something new, something borrowed, something blue ... Oh, and something in writing too.

Welcome to the world of prenuptial agreements. Usually the domain of tacky gold diggers like Anna Nicole Smith, now there is increasing interest in them in the UK.

In Australia, where I live, prenuptials are a legally binding agreement between two starry-eyed lovers entering into holy matrimony to protect their assets should either one ever forget their wedding vows. Prenuptials have always raised a few eyebrows, with concern centring on whether they are worth entering into, especially for young people. These agreements are mainly used by one person who comes into the relationship with significantly more assets than the other – as in boy meets girl, girl has a three-bedroom apartment.

In the UK, prenuptial agreements are generally not enforced in divorce courts. Those fuddy duddy old judges don't like having their hands tied when it comes to making settlements in divorce cases. About 40 per cent of marriages end in divorce, perhaps one reason why more of use are choosing to cohabit. Around 70 per cent of couples now live together before getting married, compared to just 5 per cent in the mid 1960s.

When you're married the law is pretty cut and dried when it comes to dividing up assets, and if you don't believe me ask one of your workmates who's gone through the process.

Living in sin, as granny would say

According to my grandmother, if two people are in a relationship and live together without wedding rings, they're 'living in sin', and on more than a few occasions I've had to tell her that I was keeping court with the devil due to my living arrangements.

Values are ever changing. At my age my parents were already married and had pumped out two kids – they were parents in their own right. At the same age about the most responsibility I have is watering the chilli plant that sits on my windowsill, which I still occasionally forget to nurture.

The fact is that people are delaying marriage till later in life. Instead, they're going down the somewhat more sensible route of living together before marriage. Why is it sensible? Most people who live out of home will agree that the only time you really get to see someone's true colours is after sharing a roof with them for an extended period.

'De facto' is a rather ugly term that describes two people in a rela-tionship living under the one roof. Most couples I know that live together agree that living together is a big form of commitment, and is basically the same as marriage, except for the expensive wedding, and the engagement presents.

According to National Statistics in 1965 just 5 per cent of coupled moved in together before marriage. These days that figure is about 70 per cent.

A cohabitation agreement

It's possible for a couple that are living together to draw up a legal agreement to cover what might happen to their joint possessions in the event of a break-up. Both parties would need their solicitors to advise them and the agreement should only cover significant material possessions such as property or joint investments and be unambiguously worded. It is worth remembering that agreements like this have still to be fully tested in UK courts so if in doubt, either make sure your own assets are kept entirely separate – or get married!

Sorting out your records with the shoe-box method

Record keeping, filing, sorting – I'm guessing none of these have ever been top of your to do list. Me too. Yet just like making an effort with your partner's parents can pay big dividends in the long run, so too does spending a little time making sure all your financial records are intact.

As my parents and, in later life, my former housemates will attest, I come from the college of disorganised chaos. On a good day my room often resembles an Iraqi bomb shelter, and I've been known to misplace (read: lose) everything from mobile phones to items of clothing at the drop of a hat.

So when it comes to dishing out info on cleanliness and order it's kinda like taking a cooking class with Hannibal Lecter as your teacher. One thing I do have in order however, are my financial records.

I'm going to attempt to make this as pain free as possible – really.

Step 1: Go out and buy yourself two pairs of shoes. Stilettos work well, so do sports shoes of any description.

Step 2: Take the shoes out of the box.

Step 3: Mark the box with the corresponding year. This box will be your highly non-technical yet very efficient financial affairs box for the year.

OK, let's go. Here's a brief list of things to chuck in the box as they come in:

Pension statements: Keep all the information that comes from your pension provider, and watch the pounds turn into hundreds, then into thousands, and then by the time it's worth a fortune you'll be too old to really enjoy it. Unless you're as cool as Jack Nicholson when you're sixty, then you'll no doubt put it to good use.

Student Loan statements: Save your original agreement and all of the statements the SLC throws at you just so as to ensure you don't forget that higher education isn't free anymore.

Credit card statements: Throw all your receipts of any credit card transactions and statements into the box. Occasionally take a look at your statement and see if there is anything 'priceless' on there, (except for the bill) also check to see if your card company really is helping you to 'live your dreams'.

Bank statements: Keep all your bank statements. If you're in a sadistic mood, highlight the bank charges and dream about what you'd rather have spent the money on.

Pay slips: Keep all your pay slips, as well as your end of financial year group certificate. When you become a bitter and twisted old-age pensioner, sitting there wondering why you're eating dog food in your golden years, certificates of pay are a fantastic piece of memorabilia that allow you to calculate just how much money you pissed up against a wall while you were young and carefree.

Tax stuff: Keep a copy of any returns you've filed, any tax statements you get, and any information from your accountant. Remember that beneath the monotone voice, and their fascination with deductions, accountants are people too.

Housing stuff: If you own your own home, keep a copy of the mortgage agreement, and any information you have received from your lender. Keeping this stuff will allow you to look back in twenty years and have your kids laugh at the tiny amount of money you paid for your first home. If you rent, include the tenancy agreement and inventory application, rent receipts, as well as any information from your landlord and estate agent. An optional extra is to get a photo of your landlord to put on the fridge so you never get caught on a surprise inspection.

Investing statements: Keep any paraphernalia you get relating to your investments. Even though your investments may be called 'growth income trust' – we know them by another name, MOJO baby, yeah!

Car stuff: Keep all your purchase information, including warranties, servicing information and any finance agreements. Keep any receipts from any repairs and registration papers. Keep a photo of your first car complete with fluffy dice to show your kids that your tackiness has strong roots.

Big ticket purchasing information: Keep all your warranties and receipts. If the hamburgler comes to your house and strips it clean, it's a good thing to have your receipts to prove to your insurance company that you actually had the stuff.

Internet purchases: When ordering that little nurse's uniform from www.kinky.com, it's a good idea to print out a copy of the order form until it arrives, as proof of purchase in case the goods don't arrive.

Keep throwing all this stuff into your box as it comes in. At the end of the year put the lid on it, file it away in your cupboard and go out and buy yourself another pair of shoes to start another year and repeat steps one to three.

The other shoe box that you have (remember you brought two pairs of shoes) is the Important Stuff box. Things you keep in here are:

- Passport
- Birth certificate
- Marriage certificate (then maybe ...)
- Divorce certificates
- Loan documentation
- Insurance forms
- A picture of yourself looking radiantly young and happy (see pay slips)
- Autographed poster from the housemates of Big Brother

Most of the things contained here you don't want to have to search for, especially your insurance forms – because if you ever find yourself looking for them chances are something will be rocking your karma. The same goes for the passport and birth certificate.

With the ID verification check in full force for most official documents, you'll often need these forms (not to mention the passport for that weekend trip to the Bahamas ...)

There you have it – no late nights spent itemising receipts or anal alphabetical filing. In the event of you needing to check something, it'll be all in the one place – the trusty shoe box, although it may require some digging. As a side note to this, if you are reading this and thinking, 'What a lazy son of a bitch, just set up a filing system!' my hat goes off to you for your organisational ability – you, my Jedi, are using the Force.

Property: a British Love Affair

How am I ever going to afford a house?

When people think about getting serious about their money – you know, as in doing something productive with it, invariably most of us think about property. The great British dream is steeped in owning your own little piece of this green and pleasant land. Brits are nutty about property – we speak about it, dream about it, watch crap television on it, and borrow heaps of money to attain

The downside to the property boom is that more than ever young people are being priced out of the market. In this chapter we take a look at some of the issues surrounding home ownership:

• Why property prices have hit the roof.
• What is the future for house prices? Expert commentary from rapper Will Smith.
• Apartments versus houses.

We finish the chapter with an action plan designed to get you in your first home, fast.

Turning the dream into reality

Britain has one of the highest levels of home ownership in the world. Interestingly, in many European countries home ownership doesn't have the same attraction. Europeans are less concerned with home ownership, and tend to do alternative things with their cash.

If I were a philosopher (which clearly I'm not) I could trace this back to our roots. In Australia for example, as former convicts and newly arrived settlers trying to establish themselves the first Europeans in this country found validation in establishing their own homes ... but I'm more convict than philosopher so I'll just stick to the facts.

It's undeniable that owning property is a powerful symbol, and one that most of us aspire to. The notion of property owner-ship carries with it some strong motives, and because of this purchasing a home isn't just a financial decision, it's also an emotional decision.

Your mother was right

Mothers like stability, and nothing says it more than owning your own home – it's the ticket to sitting at the big people's table and being treated as an adult. Owning your own home shows that you've been disciplined enough to save up for a deposit. It shows that you can stay in a place longer than six months. It shows that you've got an asset behind you, and that you are actually starting to get your investment program on track.

So playing the numbers game, I'm going to assume that most people reading this book either own their own home, or have plans to do so at some stage – share house living isn't that cool in your forties people, and neither is dealing with landlords for that matter.

Talk to anyone over the age of forty – or most people in a suit – and they'll no doubt advise you: 'Buy a house as soon as you can, start paying it off, it's the best investment you can make.'

While it's true that if you plan on living under a roof for the next fifty or so years, it's probably a good idea to eventually buy a house, but the notion of 'buy a house as quickly as you can and start paying it off' is based more on emotion than logic. This is a weird aspect of the financial world – there seems to be an undertone of largely condescending advice that presupposes there is just one correct path, one correct action for everyone to follow.

Life isn't always black and white – in most cases it's a mixture of both. You're an individual, on your own path, so it's beyond me (or anyone else for that matter) to dish out contrived, blanket style advice and assume that it will pertain to your specific situation.

Hey I'm not dissin' the great property dream, just merely highlighting that home ownership (as we've discussed) isn't solely a financial decision – it's an emotional one as well. Far better for me to discuss both sides of the home ownership coin and let you reach your own conclusion ...

Four walls: home or prison?

Let's take a look at some of the advantages of owning your own home, followed by some of the disadvantages.

Forced savings

Owning your home forces you to get serious about reining in your spending and to start sorting out your money situation – nothing beats regular mortgage repayments to make you save. The forced discipline of regularly paying off an asset over many years is the reason most people make money out of property over the long term.

Taxation

Entrenched in our national psyche is the great British dream of home ownership, and politicians who like being elected understand this fact and tend not to stand in its way. Because of this we have some of the juiciest property taxation structures in the Western world.

If you purchase a home and live there so it is your residence and then sell it at a profit, no capital gains tax is paid, unlike investing in shares (or property in which you don't live) where a proportion of the profit you make is taxed at your marginal tax rate.

Huh? Look, tax is boring, tax costs you money – tax sucks. Just remember this – if you sell the house you live in and make a zillion bucks profit out of it, you don't have to share it with the government, and these days pretty much everything is taxed to some degree, so it's a sweet deal.

Originality

Haven't you heard? Everyone's doing it! It's a national obsession. Take the 'hit' of home renovation and you too can spend cosy weekends at John Lewis, wild nights at Ikea – even use your hydroponics skills to grow a real vegie garden.

Owning your own home allows you to add your own personal touch to the place where you live. If you rent there's not much point in repainting your bathroom, because (a) it's not your house and (b) you're probably going to move on in 12 months or so.

King of your castle

Being the king of your castle means you're not at the mercy of a land-lord or estate agent. If you rent, your house can be sold; or your lease may not be renewed, which means that you may be forced to (involuntarily) move every couple of years.

There's also what I call the 'aggro effect' of renting – applying for properties, surprise inspections, snooty property managers and crazy landlords.

Lassie also gets a rough deal here. He may be able to save drowning kids from lakes and faithfully deliver your paper each morning, but that doesn't usually cut it with landlords, many of whom stipulate a no pet policy. Then again, I've lived in plenty of places that were home to a colony of cockroaches, as well as a family of mice, and that didn't seem to bother them.

Emotions

While it's different for everyone, most people would agree that owning a home packs an emotional punch. It's stability in your life. There's a certain sense of pride in actually owning a little chunk of Britain. It's the warm fuzzy feeling you get when you stand by the fireplace and admire the fact that you've now got something behind you that is uniquely yours.

There are always two sides to every story. On the flip side, owning a home can change your life completely

Costs

When you purchase a home there are significant upfront costs involved such as stamp duty, conveyancing and the fees associated with getting a mortgage. On the other hand, when you rent you don't pay any upkeep, which means for any repairs all you have to do is ring up your estate agent who will arrange for a handyman to fix them, and the landlord gets lumped with the bill.

You would have had to be living under a rock for the past ten years if you didn't realise that property prices have skyrocketed. In order to get a foothold in the property market, purchasing a home in any of our major cities (and increasingly regional towns), involves taking out mortgages for seriously big bucks – and a huge mortgage equals huge repayments.

I've got friends who have purchased homes, and the repayments have significantly changed their lives. I'm not talking about delaying that trip to the Bahamas; they feel it in the small ways, like fretting over going out for Sunday lunch.

Freedom

The freedom of renting enables you to pretty much pick up, pack up and go. You're not constrained by mortgage repayments, and that allows you to stay somewhere for a week, six months, a year, or five years, and always have the choice of packing up and going should you seek greener pastures, get the travel bug, or move for a job opportunity somewhere else.

When is the right time to buy?

Every now and again certain events leave a lasting impression, and play a role in shaping your perceptions. Mine occurred at a party in Sydney in January 2004. The party was rocking – a steady supply of booze, plenty of finger food, cool tunes and some damn fine eye candy thrown in to boot.

After lubricating myself with a beer at the makeshift bar and scoffing down some nachos, I joined a group of twentysomethings sitting out the back engrossed in conversation. What was the topic that had this group so transfixed? To my surprise it wasn't the usual – music, drugs, or sex. My fellow compadres were debating the topic of house prices, and the particular focus was on a guy who'd done the seemingly impossible of buying his own place, and people were literally in awe of him.

As I sat there I noticed that the people engaged in the conversation were in their mid-twenties, most had university degrees, many were earning decent cash, and through it all, home ownership was a pipe dream for all of them.

How could a group of financially independent, highly paid young people not be able to afford a dog kennel a hundred miles from the city? Warning bells started to ring inside my head. The property boom was already taking a heavy toll on me, if for nothing else than the punishing television line-up of crap home improvement shows that I was subjected to on a nightly basis. Carol Smillie had changed just one too many rooms. It was to do some detective work for my party pals and work out just what was behind this madness.

Why property prices have hit the roof

Three main factors are driving property prices to insane levels:

- Low interest rates.
- The deregulation of the finance industry.
- The Baby Boomer generation.

Interest rates—cheap money

The ultimate reality TV show these days has nothing to do with whose restaurant rules, building a resort, or singing like a budgie on prime time – it's all about interest rates. Heading the list of key players is the governor of the Bank of England, Mervyn King. He's the man with all the answers (and a damned good poker face). Next come the various economists who talk a lot but really don't know what the hell's going on, and the millions of everyday Brits whose lives hang in the balance – move over *Big Brother*!

What's the deal with interest rates? It seems that everyone is talking about them. Are they going up, down, sideways? Who cares?

In Britain, as with our daddy Mr America, we've experienced record low interest rates, the likes of which we haven't seen for decades. The reason this is important is that when interest rates are low, money is cheaper due to the smaller amount of interest paid on debt. Because people are paying less interest on debt, it encourages them to borrow more.

The problem is that interest rates don't stay low indefinitely. When interest rates start rising the opposite occurs to people with variable interest debt (as opposed to those who have locked their interest rates in at fixed rates) – the repayments start climbing ... but let's stick to the script.

Interest rates in 30 seconds

Official interest rates are often a hot topic in the media, so it's surprising just how few people understand anything about them.

The Bank of England sets interest rates, a function that is known as monetary policy'. It is an independent body, separate from the government.

I don't want to get bogged down in economic theory, so let's say the role of the Bank is kind of like the Captain on the Love Boat – it watches over everything that's going on with our economy and makes sure the ship is on the right course by controlling the money supply.

The Bank has a target to keep inflation (meaning prices rising, stay with me ...) within a band of 2–3 per cent. Other factors also influence their decisions. For example, recently we have seen the Bank lower interest rates in order to bolster a flagging economy.

Deregulation of the finance industry

Years ago if you wanted a loan you had limited choices. It was basically the big four banks and a handful of building societies. These guys were the gatekeepers of credit, and they kept their lending criteria pretty tight.

Back in the dark ages (when your parents were your age now) you had to have, like actual cash in the bank, and written documentation to prove you actually made, like money. Worst of all you had to show your potential lender you had a strong history of saving – you remember saving don't you? It's when you take a certain amount of cash and put it away so you can pay for something down the track ...

These days every man and his dog is a mortgage lender, and the competition for customers between lenders is cut-throat. Gone are the days of sucking up to your local bank manager.Today it's easier to get a loan than it is to score at a backpacker hostel.

As a result of this competition, the lending criteria for getting a loan has never been easier – we've even heard of lenders allowing you to take the 'equity' out of your car and use it as a deposit for a house!

The boom has also provided door-to-door encyclopedia salesmen with new careers as debt consultants. Sadly, most of the people calling themselves debt consultants have about as much knowledge of finance as they do about the contents of the encyclopedias they once sold, but this hasn't stopped 'debt consolidation' becoming one of the fastest growing industries of the last decade.

The duelling banjos of low interest rates and cheap and easy credit has meant that people have had access to more debt to throw at housing. How much? In July 2005 total UK personal debt broke through the £1.1 trillion barrier, up 10 per cent in just 11 short months. Personal debt is now increasing at £1 million every four minutes.

Baby Boomers

The final element in the housing boom is the Baby Boomer generation. The largest generation in history is full steam ahead for retirement; with the majority set to be kicking up their heels by the end of this decade.

The problem for the boomers is they're heading towards retirement without enough cash in the piggy bank – they wrongly assumed that the generous pension would be around to look after them as it did for their parents. Nope.

The government's coffers won't stretch far enough to keep them all in golf clubs, so they introduced Stakeholder Pensions – which is basically the government's way of telling people to look after themselves.

It's not all bad for these Baby Boomers, because even though they haven't saved much in the form of investments, most of them have adhered to that time honoured advice of 'buy a house, pay off your mortgage, it's the best investment you'll ever make'.

Putting it all together

OK, so we've got cheap money, easy credit and the biggest genera-tion on the brink of retirement. How does it pan out? Well, most Baby Boomers are looking at retirement as a way to get more in tune with dog food. Hey it's not that bad! 'Top breeders recommend it', you know.

Thank god they've paid off their mortgages ... at least their homes are secure. Then along comes sustained low interest rates that make debt a lot more affordable, closely followed by Mr Encyclopedia Salesman telling them they can 'access' the money in their paid-off home without even having to sell it! They can 'free up' their capital and use it to buy more houses. 'Have you seen the property market lately? It's booming baby!

It's the new way to become a millionaire, no a *multi* millionaire. Don't just buy one ... buy ten! Many Baby Boomers are seeing the growth in property and are buying it with their ears pinned back as a means of beefing up their meagre retirement savings.

The tide is changing; suddenly many Baby Boomers are thinking caviar instead of dog food. How simple is it? Just keep redrawing money out of their original home and keep buying more and more houses, and because rates are low, and *everyone's* in on the game, prices keep going up, giving them more profit to buy even more houses.

The problem is that things have gone a little wacko. First home-buyers – my pals at the party – have been largely driven out of the market by Baby Boomers buying up houses with a capitalistic concoction of equity and cheap debt. With so many houses being bought for investment, the rental market has been flooded with competition, which has seen rents tumble. Forget the high-brow economics people – if you're currently renting you'll no doubt have seen that there's a lot more houses/apartments to choose from, and that the rent, far from going up, in some cases is going down.

In a *rational* market when the return on an investment (rent) diminishes the price of an asset (house) comes back to earth. This hasn't happened. In most of our capital cities rental yields are at record lows.

Will Smith eloquently summarised the property conundrum in his groundbreaking hit of the late 90s, 'Boom! Shake the Room'. I happen to know Will is a dedicated property prognosticator who was delivering us his prediction for the property market in the form of woefully bad teenage rap.

Was Will on the money about it being a boom? Well, for the past few years established property owners have been falling over them-selves to get in the market, so there were more buyers than sellers – sending prices skyward. The problem is that when the *returns* of an asset move too far away from the price of an asset you have the strange phenomena of the 'bigger fool theory', as in 'Who's the bigger fool willing to pay more for this house/apartment/dog kennel?' BOOM! SHAKE-SHAKE-SHAKE THE ROOM.

Of course other factors have had an effect on the property market like City fat-cat bonuses, immigration, relatively high employment, population growth and a strong economy. However, in my view most of these have been an adjunct to the three driving factors I've explained.

First home action plan

What to do, when to do it, how to achieve it

There are a million and one shysters out there talking trash about property. Truth be known there isn't a magic formula, there's no fairy godmother handing out deposits, and no let up in house prices – yet.

Let's cut through the crap and analyse the best way to achieve the goal of home ownership.

Buying v renting

We've all heard finance people and very often real estate people come out with that old adage of 'rent is dead money'.

It's true that owning your own home makes good sense – I don't think anyone could argue that paying off a mortgage for 30 years and ending up with a house beats the absolute pants off paying rent for 30 years and ending up with nothing. But the right advice is whatever is right for you. Certainly at some stage you should look at purchasing a home, and the common assumption that you should save up for a deposit as quickly as possible is followed by the same conventional wisdom that says those who do it are the smart ones – while the rest of us are out pissing money up against a wall, they're painting theirs.

The flipside of that argument is the trade-off of going into debt to buy something is paying for it. 'What's the point of scrimping and saving to get a deposit,' I hear you cry, 'only to get a mortgage and have to continue watching every penny in order to pay it off?' All the money in the world can't buy back your youth.

The property boom has thrown a couple of curve balls at would-be first homebuyers. If you have digested the factors that are driving the boom you may be starting to question the logic of paying inflated prices in order to get set in the market. Remember, if you saddle yourself for a huge loan for a property and the property's price drops, you still have to pay off the loan – it's called negative equity and it occurs when the value of the loan is more than the value of the property.

The second curve ball is the sheer amount of debt that you have to assume in order to get a roof over your head to buy property. Whichever way you look at it, it's a huge financial commitment that will certainly change the way you live over the next ten (or so) years.

You're unique, treading your own path, so at the end of the day the choice of home ownership depends largely on what stage of life you're at, and what your priorities are. Buying a home is something we should all strive to do at some stage. By following the principles in this book, when the time is right you'll have the skills needed to meet the challenge.

We're in the midst of the biggest property boom in the last hundred years. No-one knows when it will end, but history has proved that every boom, be it in tulips, property, stocks, or Michael Jackson paraphernalia, is always followed by a bust.

History also tells us that in the heat of the boom most people get caught up in it and can't see the forest for the trees – remember the dotcom millionaire whose company was the biggest and best thing ever? He's running an internet café in Milton Keynes, spending his days surfing for porn.

There are those experts who say that property will have a 'soft' landing – if it does it's probably one of the few times in history that a rampant boom has ever trickled out and not hurt anyone.

Sooner or later interest rates will go up and people will face a dual reality: property prices *do* go down and interest rates *do* go up, and following that logic, the debt people have loaded up on has to be repaid.

Rents are historically cheap due to an increase in properties being purchased for investment purposes rather than by owner occupiers. As a result of this there are more rental properties on the market, and more properties means more competition, which leads to stressed-out landlords lowering their rents in an attempt to attract a tenant.

You can take advantage of this to screw your landlord and put the money you save towards paying off any debts you have, or if you are a savvy Barefooter who doesn't play the debt game, combine your cash with some Barefoot investing strategies to turbo charge saving for a home deposit.

I have a sneaking suspicion that property prices may come down to earth before the last of the Baby Boomers head to the coast. So, sit back and relax, 'before the whole shithouse goes up in flames', to quote Jim Morrison from a Doors concert held in Los Angeles almost thirty years ago.

Getting a deposit

No matter what way you look at it, saving for a home deposit is a daunting task. With the average home costing at least £170 000 (and a lot more in many parts of London), coming up with the 10–15 per cent you need to get going is a lot of crackers in anyone's language. Let's look at the different options available.

It's time to get on the front foot and get a realistic look at how much you're going to have to set aside. You do this by looking at properties that are within your price range (even if it's a couple of years down the track). The reason you should start looking at different properties isn't just to start getting a handle on the market. It's also important to make the savings goal real to you. Hey, I'm not advocating the psychic approach of Derek in *Most Haunted*, but I do believe that focusing on the end result helps to direct your thoughts and energy into achieving your goals.

Now maybe it's an inner-city loft apartment, a three-bedroom semi on the outskirts of town, or maybe it's a McMansion in the burbs.

You're probably thinking I'll be able to give you a host of practical advice on the best areas to look at, the advantages of being close to amenities, and cool DIY tips on renovating. Let's get one thing straight. I'm not Alan Titchmarsh. I get my kicks from the market, not the garden, and certainly not from sanding a wall (maybe 'laying carpet' but that's another book). If you're wanting DIY tips turn on the TV (any channel, any night) and watch a home improvement show.

As for tips on where you should buy? Personally my living arrangements are chosen based on proximity to licensed drinking venues, restaurants, and work. What the hell do I know? I'm a stockbroker for godsakes!

Although one thing I can help you with is determining how much you'll need to save up to get your pad, and helping you with strategies to get you there quick. By looking at the general prices of properties you can afford you'll be able to see approximately how much you're going to have to save, and set your target figure.

OK, it's example time. Let's just say that you're looking at a flat that's around the £250 000 mark. You'll need about 15 per cent of the purchase price to cover the deposit, stamp duty and fees. Fifteen per cent of £250 000 means that you're going to have to save up roughly £37 500. That's a significant amount of money. If you saw £37 500 on the side of the road you wouldn't kick it down a drainpipe now would you?

There are volumes of information on how to save for a deposit, most of it written by middle-aged authors who saved for a deposit before you or I were born, who don't have student loan debts, and who don't appear to have a social life of any description. Some of the stuff I've read is the type of 'advice' your parents would dole out.

There are no easy answers to saving for a home deposit. As we've established, it's something most of us will have to do at some point in our life. The Barefoot approach is to recognise that if buying a property is your goal, its time to get serious, and there's no room for half measures. If purchasing a home is your number one priority, your *other* number one priority can't be a month's holiday in Australia nor can it be a mahogany designer desk.

The first thing that I would suggest is re-reading the budgeting section of this book, and paying particular attention to the envelope and separate bank accounts technique, which will enable you to take control of your money.

You're also going to have to develop an effective strategy about where you place your savings to exploit the best ways to grow it before using it as a deposit. There are a few options you have which are all dependent on how long away your goal of home ownership is. If you are looking to purchase a home in the next five years or so, I would caution against putting that money in the stock market, its just too volatile to predict over the short term, and the last thing you want is to lose money you need.

This leaves you with interest-bearing investments, the likes of which we spoke about in the banking chapter. E accounts offer a great rate of interest and allow you to have your money at call if you run into trouble.

For those people who don't plan on taking the plunge until we're safely in the 2010s, the share market may well be the place for you. Luckily this is an investing book, and hopefully you've already read the fairly spiffy investing primer.

Plant your foot on the accelerator

As we discussed earlier, the current state of the housing market has meant that the rental market has been seriously oversupplied. If you rent, use this to your advantage, negotiate down your rent, or move to a cheaper suburb (or both).

The name of the game is lowering your overheads, stretching your dollar further and directing these savings to an effectively implemented investing strategy so that you can achieve your goal quicker.

If you're starting at zero (well almost zero), saving for a deposit can seem like an unattainable goal. Bullshit. I'm not Mr Motivator. But if you want it badly enough you can make it happen. Millions of people do it every day, and you're no different to them. All it takes is determination, and the guts to see it through.

Let's have a look at a few different strategies that could speed up the process to getting you into a home:

- Taking a second job
- Getting a leg up from your family
- Going 'Dutch' with a mate

Taking a second job

Often financial advisers suggest getting an extra part-time job, in addition to full-time employment. Straight off the bat, it's a personal choice and depends on how badly and how quickly you want to make things happen for you.

For me personally, I'm already working forty to fifty hours a week. Most people I know who are starting out in their careers are working the same sorts of hours as me, and the thought of taking on a part-time job where you're going to be hit with second job tax (which takes away up to 40 per cent of whatever you earn) is pretty damned hard-core.

For my vote, there's a better way. You're only young once, and you don't want to be spending your 'fun years' working your guts out, just so you can get a huge mortgage and keep working your butt off. Let's be practical: you've got to have some 'you' time, you *need* a social life. It can't be all about the money, after all you only live once.

My alternative to a second job is to look at the opportunities you have in your present career. Look at ways of getting a promotion, and then bank that promotion. Start to investigate ways to climb up the ladder where you can make the time you spend in your career really start to pay off.

Getting a leg up from your family

Do you remember your grandparents' birthdays? Have your parents forgiven you for those teenage angst years? Got a rich uncle, aunty, or significant other? Are you in your forties and still living in the family nest?

For most young people, the time they need a financial leg up isn't at the age of forty when (or if) the inheritance cheque comes. The time you can really benefit from a transfer of family wealth is when you're just starting out.

Feel free to use that line of argument with family members. The answer will be determined on the financial situation of the person you ask, and your relationship with them. Nothing ventured, nothing gained.

A recent survey found that almost 90 per cent of parents would try to help their children purchase a home if they were in the financial position to do so. 'Being in a financial position to do so' being the key words. These days, the tradition of helping your offspring into a property has become increasingly difficult in the wake of soaring property values.

The traditional way that parents have helped their children get a foothold in the property market is by contributing to the deposit, or in some cases by offering guarantees on the family home.

The big banks are starting to wake up to this trend, and are now offering standardised products to make the process of assisting immediate family members into a property easier. The general features of these products are likely to change at whim, but the basics involve a family member acting as guarantor (providing security for a loan), and also the option of a family member providing assistance with mortgage repayments. Beware, though: these packages are not exactly risk free.

Most of these products involve a family member putting their home on the line to help you get yours. If things go wrong (which court transcripts indicate they have on many occasions) your relative could lose her house. That's certainly not cool. I don't like taking too much risk with my own money, let alone with a family member who has been good enough to help me out.

It's important to note that different lenders have different policies regarding your parents helping you out. Ultimately, you're the one who is signing on the dotted line, and regardless how much a loving family member gives you, most lenders still want to ensure that you are capable to finance the home and make the repayments.

Investigate all your family support options, but at the end of the day, if you can't afford a house without large amounts of assistance, that's probably a good indication that now isn't the right time.

Going 'Dutch' with a mate

Another strategy that you may speed up the process of you owning a home is going 'Dutch' with a mate. If you've lived with a friend for a while and you get along well, you may want to investigate pooling your financial resources and purchase a house together. The legal term for this is 'tenants in common'.

Tenants in common is an agreement whereby you and another person can purchase a house and split the costs (50/50 or whatever the financial agreement between the two of you is). This can help you to purchase a home a lot quicker than struggling away on your lonesome.

One of the most important things to remember is that each person on the mortgage is 'joint and severally liable' to pay the mortgage payments. If one party doesn't pay their share, the lender will chase you for the lot.

If you've ever tried to split a phone bill in a share house, you'll no doubt understand that going into a deal such as this can quickly turn into *Nightmare on Elm Street.* If buying a home 'tenants in common' sounds enticing, it's essential to ensure you have a clear and accurate picture of the person's finances you'll be entering into the deal with. Issues such as shared financial maintenance of the property and having an effective escape clause should be written into a contract between the parties.

Before you go down this route, I would strongly advise that you talk to your accountant, and obtain legal advice. At the end of the day, if your share house mate annoys you, it's not that difficult to get out of the lease and move on. When you own an asset together, things can get a little tricky.

How much can I borrow?

These days prices are quoted using single figures – as in *four* or *seven* (hundred thousand). It's a huge amount of money whichever way you look at it. Unless Bill Gates is your sugar daddy you're going to have to go to a financial institution to get a leg up.

I remember sitting down talking to my parents about how they got a loan for our first family home. They told me that even though they had a deposit of 30 per cent, and had a regular savings history with that building society, they still had to beg the manager to lend them the money.

Back in those days, the building society manager was the 'man' (or woman). In Britain 35 years ago there were only a handful of building societies to choose from if you wanted a mortgage. The big banks didn't do mortgages. This lack of choice meant that they could be highly selective about who they lent money to.

In Australia, you could borrow from a bank, but that didn't make it any easier. My parents had to show the bank manager their marriage certificate as a way of proving they were worthy of a loan – definitely a raw deal for the *Queer Eye for the Straight Guy* crew.

All this changed back in the early 80s, when the government decided to deregulate the finance industry. This meant the industry was opened up to more competition for the big four banks, and ultimately more choice for consumers.

Deregulation has been fantastic for consumers: banking costs have come down and there are now a variety of different products and banks to meet the demands of consumers.

Deregulation has also opened up a whole raft of, shall we say, less than honourable lenders. There are literally hundreds of stories where lenders have misled and deceived in order to get people to sign on the bottom line. The competition to sign people up in the heat of the property boom has also meant that some lenders have lowered their selection criteria in order to attract more customers.

At the end of the day lending money is a business. Lenders are in the biz of lending money for a profit and the biggest difference today, as opposed to previous generations, is much more choice, and more onus on the consumer to make informed decisions.

If I had a dollar for every time I was asked, 'How much do I need to buy a house?', I could probably buy my own property with cash. The answer depends on where you want to live and what you want to buy.

I would suggest you don't go for the McMansion straight off the bat. If you're like most people you're going to have to trade up several times before *Ideal Home* start knocking on your door to do a photo shoot. In the words of Ali G, 'keep it real'.

Finance books tend to show their age by talking about houses worth £75 000. In major cities, that would be lucky to get you a one-bedroom cardboard box. In this day and age, average properties are around £170 000 or more if you are living in London or other major cities in the UK.

Choose a property that you feel comfortable with, both in living arrangements and sticker price. Above all make sure you can comfortably make the repayments and still have some semblance of a life.

Even though I advise saving 15 per cent of the value of the home, there are lenders who'll let you borrow 95 per cent, sometimes even 100 per cent, of the value of the property. In these cases you're going to have to pay mortgage insurance. Mortgage insurance protects the lender if you default on your repayments and it usually costs around 1.5 per cent of the value of the loan.

For example, if you put down £15 000 on a £150 000 property, the mortgage insurance of 1.5 per cent is going to be about £2250 and that's an upfront cost. To get around mortgage insurance you're probably going to have to keep your borrowing below 85 per cent of the value of the property.

Apartment or house?

I've lived in apartments, houses and places that resembled the stable where baby Jesus was born. From a financial point of view, which is better? I learnt this lesson at a shrine to manhood – a pub in Sydney.

Apartments are usually cheaper than houses. There is also the possibility of purchasing an apartment closer to the action (whatever action it is you're looking for) for considerably less than a house would cost you.

As with everything in property it comes back to it being a personal decision that only you can make. Personally I love the idea of having a backyard big enough to have a BBQ, a dog, and a vegie patch – the trade-off may be having to live a bit further from the action.

Working as a barman in a pub in the docklands area of Sydney I learnt a thing or two about property. Like most of Sydney there had been an explosion in prices there. One of my regulars, Jack, was a bloke nearing sixty who was invariably perched in his regular stool each time I started a shift. Jack wasn't a bad bloke. Sure, he always complained about his arthritis, and the fact that there was never anything good on the television – hence the reason he was always at the pub.

Jack wasn't what you call an astute investor, by his own admission he didn't have money to go 'throwing about the place'. But, about thirty years ago he did something that proved he had the sort of investment nous to rival the best of the pros. Jack bought a huge block of land, right bang in the middle of docklands – it's now valued at several million Aussie dollars!

Over a beer one day Jack explained his rather simple property philosophy: 'They're not making any more land.' What he was getting at is the value of owning land. The house you build on the land, no matter how good, will one day fall down, but the land underneath will be the thing that appreciates over time (read: go up in price).

Always remember, the same goes for buying an apartment in a huge high-rise. Often only a small percentage of your purchase price is attributed to the value of the land underneath. In a falling market, it should come as no surprise that inner-city apartments are often hardest hit – they tend to be large high-rise complexes built on relatively small parcels of land.

Negotiating a mortgage

One of my favourite lines in the legendary movie *Wall Street* is 'there's too much cheap money sloshing around the country' and that is certainly true today. These days it's easier to get a loan than a lap dance in Soho. There's a whole raft of lenders out there happy to lend you cash, because they are in the business of selling money. In this age of technology, bank managers have been replaced with computers. Most banks now have electronic scoring systems to verify your credit worthiness.

In the old days if the bank manager didn't like the look of your haircut you wouldn't get your loan. Nowadays it's been stream-lined (a fancy name for people being replaced by computers) and there's a point system based on parameters the lending institution has established to determine how much money you can borrow.

It's time to dispel a common delusion among home loan seekers: just because a lender will approve a limit that could safely cure the Third World of poverty, doesn't mean that you should take it.

There's no free lunch. You're not at school anymore. Lending is a business, and they're not in the business of wiping your arse. Don't expect a lender to look out for you anymore than you'd expect a car salesman to get you a car that's 'right for you'. What they'll lend you is one side of the equation, the calculations you've made about how much you can afford to repay is ultimately what should guide your decisions.

When things go belly-up

People are most optimistic when they have a goal, especially if that goal is a two-bedroom brick veneer with parquetry floors.

Most mortgage lenders these days have financial calculators that help you to work out your repayments. My advice? Play around with the numbers. Add 3 per cent to the current interest rate and work out your repayments. Don't say it won't ever happen – in the early 90s borrowers were paying 17 per cent interest on their money (I bet they didn't expect it to happen either).

Murphy's Law says that whatever can go wrong, will go wrong. At this stage of the game (late 2005), the betting man is putting his chips on the direction of interest rates rising in the future. If you're taking out a 30-year loan and at least part of it is set at a variable rate, you'd expect that over the next thirty years interest rates will go up, down and sideways.

When entering into a contract to borrow heaps of money it makes a ton of sense to ask a few 'what if' questions.

- What if interest rates climb?
- What if I break my leg and can't work?
- What if I suffer from premature balding?

If you can answer these questions you're on the right track to making an informed decision where you've thought everything out. You'll note that I haven't included information about different mortgages, mainly because they change too often, and that's beyond the scope of this book.

Once you have saved enough money for a deposit, you're comfortable with the market, and have found a pad, I'd suggest you seek impartial advice on the best mortgage for you.

Preparation for the Debt Olympics

Before you look for a mortgage there are a few things that you really should hone in on to maximise your chances of getting the best loan for you.

1. Apply to one of the three main credit checking companies to get your credit report: Go through it with a fine-tooth comb to ensure that there's no nasty surprises in there to hinder your chances of getting a loan.

2. Employment stability: When applying for a loan make sure your employment is stable, or can be verified as stable.

3. Pay off debt: You'll no doubt know that I'm a fan of paying off all debt. Carrying debt may lower the amount of money that you can borrow.

Give me a home!

After reading this section you may be starting to think that I'm anti-property. That couldn't be further from the truth. In my heart of hearts I'm a contrarian. Pretty simple really: sell when people are buying and buy when people are selling. Sounds logical on paper wouldn't you agree?

I want a home. I have a deposit. I'm sick of renting. I can't stand my landlord. I'm waiting. Patiently.

Barefoot Entrepreneurs

In the final chapter, we're going to meet young people – Barefoot Entrepreneurs – who started with nothing and used their ideas, youth, passion and creativity to carve out business fortunes. We profile Natalie Bloom, founder of Bloom cosmetics and Peter Alexander of Peter Alexander Sleepwear fame.

We also look at some of the advantages of youth when it comes to setting up a business, and why *right now* may be the best time for you to embark on your own adventure.

Wage slavery

Monday I'll have Friday on my mind
EASY BEATS

I've had many jobs throughout my life, but it wasn't until full-time employment hit that I realised the tag 'employee' didn't suit.

Each morning I'd get up and catch the bus into the Sydney CBD around 8.30 am. The bus stopped at Wynyard station and the doors would open to the hurly-burly of office workers, coffee in hand, head down, scurrying to get to their offices by 9 am. The sight of thousands of people pushing their way through the city streets reminded me of rounding up sheep on the farm.

I had a morning ritual, which after a while I could do with my eyes closed. Grab a coffee on the way (latte, two sugars thanks), keep my head down until I got to my huge office tower, get in the lift, hit level 10, log onto my computer, check my emails, and then do largely repetitive, same-as-yesterday-and-the-day-before work. Watch the clock. Lunch! Back to work. Watch the clock. 5 pm. Home time! Join the sheep, head down, catch the bus home. Repeat. Repeat. Repeat.

There was little room for creativity, little room for making a difference (unless the 'big' manager gave it his stamp of approval). I was given an operations manual on the tasks I was to perform, which I was periodically assessed against for HR appraisals.

A wise man once told me that one of the dynamics of a work environment was it forced you to interact with people you ordinarily wouldn't bother with. He also said that it was an excellent chance to forge friendships with people you otherwise wouldn't have anything in common with.

Maybe that wise old man was working at MI5 and sipping martinis with James Bond after work, or perhaps he did a stint at the United Nations where he would cadge smokes off Kofi Annan and talk about the Middle East peace process over a friendly ciggie – whatever the case 'forging relationships with people you otherwise wouldn't come into contact with' wasn't the right advice for my job.

I could tell that most of the people I worked with had been there far too long. They were effectively trapped. They hated their jobs (and most of their co-workers), but had been there so long they didn't know any better. Instead of quitting and treading their own path, they remained there stuck in a rut, complaining incessantly and doing their best to work as little as possible. It was like being back in high school again. There were cliques where you were either in, or out. 'Are you friends with this person, because they get along well with the boss'. 'That person is a troublemaker! He won't last'. Office politics did my head in. Just like a man wearing mustard pants and a pink shirt, it was time for me to come out of the closet – I had become a wage slave.

Corporate capers

Don't for a moment think I'm dissing modern-day corporate life. It's just that it's not my cup of tea, or latte for that matter. I have friends who absolutely thrive on the challenge of the organisational environment. Many of them are stimulated by the roles they perform – they wouldn't change their careers for anything. There is no correct path, the only right answer is the one inside your head. As they say, it's a case of different horses for different courses.

The entrepreneurial spirit is something that's in my blood. My father quit school at the age of fifteen to work at a service station in a little country town. To cut down on costs he lived in a caravan out the back of his boss's house. It worked: a few years later he bought the fuel distribution business and later added the school bus. Then he tried his hand at a freight-moving business and, more recently, a camera shop.

At some point most of us have dreamed about leaving our salaried positions to start a business venture that allows us to use our creativity and build something that is unique, call the shots and make a fortune in the process. The thing that snaps most people back to reality is the downside – it's a well-known fact that most businesses fail within the first twelve months and in many cases leave the owners flat broke. There are many risks inherent in leaving the safety net of a reliable income.

Because I have been exposed to many different family businesses over the years, the thought of peril or riches has never really influenced my thinking.

My earliest memories of having family businesses was that Dad was always there to kick the footy with me, pick me up from school or take me fishing. While other dads had salary-driven jobs with the restrictions of set hours and fixed holidays, my father had the freedom to plan his day the way it best suited him. It was this freedom that attracted me – the money and the limelight came a distant second.

Young, restless and successful

This hasn't been written as a 'how to' chapter. There's not a book in the world that can give you a guaranteed path to becoming an entrepreneur – actually there are a few, but they're up there with guys selling their secrets on 'wealth creation'.

There are many people who have had tremendous success by buying into a proven business franchise like McDonald's, Thorntons or Card Connection, just like there are people who have done fantastically well opening up, say a laundromat, but unless you have a passion for cleaning clothes, we're focusing on something altogether different. My father had a habit of saying that plenty of people go into business to make money, only to find that they've really bought a 100-hour-a-week job.

A Barefoot Entrepreneur symbolises everything we've covered in this book. They're young, passionate about what they do, daring to be different, smart with their money and treading their own unique path.

In the book *Getting Rich Your Own Way* author Srully Blotnick writes about a fascinating research project he conducted on 1500 middle-class Americans. In the initial interview his researchers probed their feelings towards money, and whether they had chosen their occupations and interests based on the potential to make a lot of money or on genuine satisfaction with the task at hand.

After twenty years the surviving interviewees were re-interviewed to see how they had fared. Blotnick and his researchers discovered that 83 of the 1500 people had become millionaires.

Now here's the interesting part – of those 83 millionaires, none came from the group who said their careers would be based on trying to make as much cash as possible. They all came from the small group of respondents who had chosen their careers based on what they loved.

Blotnick later commented that, 'the fact remains that the overwhelming majority of people who have become wealthy have become so thanks to work they found profoundly absorbing ... The long-term study of people who eventually became wealthy clearly reveals that their 'luck' arose from the accidental dedication they had to an area that they enjoyed'. It certainly reinforces that old saying, 'do what you love and the money will follow'.

My radio program has me interviewing highly successful people of all ages.

One of the common themes I've picked up in nearly every person I've interviewed is a passion for their particular business coupled with a strong level of self-belief.

It's certainly true that most of these business stars – people like Anita Roddick, founder of the Body Shop or Sir Richard Branson of Virgin – didn't start out with millions of pounds at their disposal. They built their empires one brick at a time. How many times do you think these three were told by their friends or family that they were too young, or that they didn't have enough capital behind them, or that they couldn't possibly compete against the giants in their particular market?

Branson went from owning a tiny student record mail-order business to owning a conglomerate that spans the globe, employing thousands of people. How many people would have thought a skinny kid from London who dropped out of school at fifteen would go on to become a billionaire? Branson obviously did.

In the end no-one knows what you're capable of achieving, and even if they did there'd still be people ready to tell you that it's impossible. A strong self-belief is your passport to where you want to go.

No-one can possibly achieve any real and lasting success or 'get rich' in business by being a conformist
J. PAUL GETTY

Happy days

Am I painting too rosy a picture of life as a small business owner? Surely we all know the bloke down the road who runs the fish and chip shop who works twelve hours a day, seven days a week! There's no kicking the footy happening there – the only time he does anything resembling a fishing trip with his kids is when he's cooking one in the deep fryer! Sure there are people who end up being a slave to their business, to the detriment of their family and social lives, but that's definitely not my focus.

On my radio show we do a segment called the Barefoot Salute where we salute young people who have gone out and started up a business that they feel passionate about. In the past we've met a young guy that started his own fashion label, lots of people who have started their own music labels, a girl who founded her own magazine, and guys that have started their own restaurants and nightclubs.

Sure they worked insane hours, and many of them had sacrificed everything to keep their vision going. For these guys, it wasn't about the cash (most of them were still in the start-up phase). They all had one thing in common – they were passionate about what they were doing. They had the opportunity to build something unique – something that wasn't there before, and they were able to fill that niche with their creativity and strength of character to make it a success.

Triple M—Mortgage, Marriage and Midgets

Barefoot Entrepreneurs highlight how young people have stepped out and chosen to build a career out of doing something they love. Young entrepreneurs are often put up on a pedestal by the media and held in awe by the people around them.

While I'm not the type of guy who's going to knock anyone for getting out and doing what they love, the idea that young people are somehow at a disadvantage in starting up a new venture is ridiculous. When you think about it, who is more likely to be able to throw caution to the wind and stake hard-earned cash on a dream? People in their twenties and thirties, or older people who have to deal with the Triple Ms (Marriage, Mortgage and Midgets)?

I've always thought that it's much easier to follow a dream if you're the only one relying on the outcome. I reckon if you've got a fully functioning 'seventh heaven' type family situation, you're either sticking with the safety net of the salary, or else you're taking a huge bet that not only affects you, but your whole family.

When young Melbourne design graduate Natalie Bloom started her cosmetics business, she didn't have these hassles but building a successful business actually gave her time later in life to devote to her family.

Let a million faces Bloom: cosmetics creator Natalie Bloom

The cosmetics industry generates billions in profits each year. The companies that rule the industry do so with an iron fist, spending a fortune on advertising in an attempt to convince women that their products will help them win the fight against the 'seven signs of ageing'. Their strategy relies heavily on the relentless message that their lipstick will transform its wearer into something close to the Hollywood starlet the company has paid the equivalent of Cambodia's national debt to feature in its ads. The companies that dominate the industry, like Chanel, Revlon, Mac, L'Oreal, Clinique and the like, spend millions of pounds protecting their market share.

You'd think that trying to compete with these monoliths would be as distant a hope as establishing a permanent ceasefire in the Middle East. But it doesn't hurt to dream does it?

In the early 90s in a leafy suburb of Melbourne, twenty-three-year-old Natalie Bloom had just finished her degree in graphic design. Natalie's a self-confessed 'girls' girl'. Like many women in their early twenties she had an eye for fashion and make-up – so much so that she played around with making cool lip gloss for her friends, using only natural ingredients, and experimenting with different textures, scents and finishes.

A little naivety goes a long way

Showing the unique combination of naivety and self-confidence common to so many young entrepreneurs, Natalie made a bold decision: she would try to make a living out of her cosmetics hobby. She was fresh out of university, with no professional experience in making cosmetics, and virtually zero cash. But she had some gentle encouragement from her friends (who loved her creations) and the desire to make this a full-time gig.

Bearing in mind that she would be competing with multinational corporations with million pound advertising campaigns, established distribution networks, thousands of employees and billions of pounds in capital, how many people would have backed her?

'I think starting my business at a young age was definitely an advantage – I had a certain naivety about me, I didn't know it couldn't be done!', she says.

Just ten years later Natalie's business, Bloom Cosmetics, is an international success. It employs a staff of thirty and Bloom products are used by millions of women all over the world.

Like our other Barefoot Entrepreneurs Natalie used her individual style, street smarts and youth to build a unique company from the ground up, and in the process broke all the traditional rules that the big companies play by.

Bloom's competitors had a vast supply of money to throw at advertising, and the industry rule of thumb was to spend millions of pounds paying celebrities to endorse their products (think Elizabeth Hurley as the face of Estee Lauder). Natalie took a new direction. Using her skills in graphic design, Natalie worked with an illustrator to create Miss Bloom, a funky character that became the 'face' of Bloom cosmetics. In Natalie's words, the fictional Miss Bloom is a 'sassy woman in her twenties, with an Audrey Hepburn sense of style'.

Natalie also understood that in order for her company to succeed, her products had to be top quality – something that has never been compromised. She took the view that the temptation to cut corners on quality may have helped her limited budget in the short term, but eventually would have undermined what she was trying to achieve.

Natalie stuck by her belief that her path to business success and an independent career was twofold: delivering quality products made from high-grade natural ingredients and packaging them distinctly using the funky Miss Bloom as the company mascot. 'In the early days I had no family to support, and no huge overheads, so I was able to keep my expenses down,' she says.

To this day Bloom Cosmetics has never paid for an advertisement in a glossy mag or on television – not that it has mattered. The products have been so successful that the company has received promotion that money can't buy – an army of fans that reads like a who's who of Hollywood, all happy to spread the word on how much they love Bloom's cosmetics. From Kylie to Cameron Diaz, Britney Spears to the editors of *In Style*, people have taken notice – and the company has boomed.

Today Bloom Cosmetics is an Australian success story, founded by a young woman passionate about cosmetics who backed her belief that women would love quality products.

With her dedicated team Natalie is now in the enviable position of being able to afford to slow down her career to spend more time with her young family, at a time when many of her friends' careers are just starting to speed up. Natalie's success has meant that she has financial success and, more importantly, the freedom to choose how she spends her time.

Turning youth to your advantage

Speak to any marketeer worth their weight in Doritos and they'll tell you the most lucrative group of consumers are people aged 16 to 25. The bulk of marketing money is spent trying to lure people in this demographic to purchase their wares.

In a bizarre case of irony there are thousands of forty and fifty-year-old marketeers, managers and entrepreneurs all trying to get a handle on the latest trends and products that will appeal to the 'young generation'. If that's the case, and it is, why not turn the situation around and celebrate your youth as the greatest asset you have in your business armoury?

Pyjama king Peter Alexander

Nowhere is the principle of turning your youth to an advantage better illustrated than in Peter Alexander's rise to the top of the sleepwear industry. Peter credits his success with observing and quizzing the sleeping habits of his twentysomething friends, which allowed him to effectively outmanoeuvre competing retail giants. As is the case with many talented young people, Peter used his youth, and understanding of the market, to spot a niche that the fiercely competitive fashion industry had overlooked.

Says Peter: 'I would ask girlfriends of mine, 'what type of pyjamas do you wear?' Invariably most of them said that they didn't like what was on offer in the women's department – most of them purchased their PJs from men's stores.' Investigating further, Peter looked at what the standard lines of pyjamas on offer were on at that time for women. 'They were either virginal house on the prairie or downright slutty,' he says. 'There was nothing in the middle like men's pyjamas with a feminine touch.'

At age twenty-three, Peter was your typical twentysomething – working (and partying) in a nightclub, as well as working in what Peter describes as a 'dead-end retail job'. But he always had his sights on succeeding at something – at that stage he just wasn't sure what it was.

Peter's career in retail wasn't the typical routine of trying to convince customers that their arse really did look good in the pants they were trying on, while dancing to music pumped out by night-club-strength speakers. Peter found a passion, and he is quick to point out that it wasn't a dream of becoming the next Giorgio Armani, (to this day he doesn't consider himself a fashion designer). He was not so interested in the aesthetics of design and focused instead on merchandising and sales of his sleepwear.

Without a university education to fall back on, Peter used the next few years as a quasi-university degree, learning everything he could about marketing and merchandising. His dedication and skill saw him rise to the position of state visual merchandise manager of a leading retailer, Sportsgirl.

On a holiday in Hong Kong, Peter spotted a pair of pyjamas that were exactly what he'd envisioned: 'They were adorable – feminine and sexy, I had to have them,' he says. Peter had been a hit working for a national retailer with deep pockets, but it was time to raise the bar and test his skills by marketing his very own range of pyjamas. Overnight, Peter Alexander Sleepwear was born.

You'd think that since Peter was supplying a niche product that had the potential to be a huge hit that he'd have the big guns of the industry beating a path to his door – not so. His first foray into landing a big deal was with retailer David Jones but it didn't go as smoothly as planned. 'They hated them,' he says. 'The senior buyer told me to stop wasting her time, and that I had absolutely no idea about retailing.'

Rival retailer Myer was a little warmer to the idea and agreed to take a small order of Pete's PJs. True to Peter's hunch, the pyjamas were a hit with women and suddenly the notoriously fickle world of retailing started to take notice. Myer was so happy with the brisk sales that they made a huge order – 2000 pairs of pyjamas.

All indications were that Peter Alexander Sleepwear was on its way up ... then disaster struck. Myer cancelled its order at the last minute, leaving 2000 pairs of pyjamas unpaid for. Says Peter: 'I was absolutely hysterical. At that stage I was still operating out of my mother's garage, and we had PJs everywhere – wall to wall!'

Things looked bad for the business. He had no way of selling all the stock, and paying the supplier had sapped his finances. At the eleventh hour Peter decided to take his last A$10 000 and place an advertisement in *Cleo*, offering the leftover PJs via mail order. He was able to sell the clothes at a lower cost than the store price because there was no retail margin on top.

The decision was a stroke of brilliance – as soon as the ad was placed, the phone started ringing off the hook. Peter was flooded with requests from eager customers placing orders for his PJs.

Until disaster struck Peter had never thought of selling his product through mail order – but it's a good thing he did. To date Peter Alexander Sleepwear has 120 000 customers on its mailing list and last year the company turned over A$15 million dollars worth of PJs.

Peter Alexander Sleepwear has now been acquired by retailing powerhouse Just Jeans group, but Peter still plays an active role in the company's activities. Having learned the lessons that made the company great, he's certainly not about to change the formula. 'A lot of water has passed under the bridge since I started the company when I was twenty-three – I'm getting close to being forty now, but I still believe that forty-year-olds can't dictate what young people want. Product decisions at Peter Alexander Sleepwear will always be made by our target customers – women in their twenties.'

My Story

As you've no doubt worked out by now, I have a passion for teaching people about money. I'm sure it came as no surprise to my old school teachers that I'd entered the world of high finance.

I was seriously interested in investing from an abnormally young age. When my mates were stealing their old man's *Playboy*s, I was stealing my Dad's *Your Money Weekly*. As I began reading about finance I found that everything was written for old people, and most of it was so dry it felt like your mouth first thing on a Sunday morning.

Then it hit me. Could I combine my love of investing with my passion for helping people my own age? More than that, could I do it in a way that was fun and exciting? Could I turn finance on its head and present it differently to anything else out there?

I had found a niche. I set out to create and fill it.

I decided to start *The Barefoot Investor* radio program. I wanted the show to be attractive to young people, with an easygoing format, so I developed the program with the idea of indulging my love of talking to people about their finances but not being over-the-top about it. We would play some cool tunes and have some laughs along the way. But before I'd even started the critics were on to me. Most people thought I was completely crazy. *'A young persons guide to finance? But kids don't have any money!'*. *'Nice idea, but no-one under the age of thirty-five is going to listen to you!'*. Or my favourite: *'Finance is boring ... '* If I had a quid for every time someone told me I couldn't pull it off, I'd have a nice car by now.

After repeatedly being told that *The Barefoot Investor* was doomed to fail from people with the 'best intentions' who were 'just trying to look out for me', I decided that if *The Barefoot Investor* was ever going to make an impact we had to be on the airwaves.

Next stop the Student Youth Network (SYN) in my hometown of Melbourne. The station is better known for its techno than technical investing, so you can imagine my proposal for a finance program was treated with raised eyebrows.

For some reason the station took a chance on me, and Barefoot radio was born. The next round of knocks came in the form of, *'A radio show? What the hell are you going to talk about?'*, and *'Who wants to listen to a finance show anyway?'*. By far my favourite remark was, *'You'll never get good guests on student radio'*.

Right from the start I was determined to make the Barefoot Investor completely different to any other financial show. Eminem, Powderfinger, and the Beastie Boys rode shotgun on the show. We delivered practical information to young people in a style that had never been done before – from doing an investment analysis of my sex life to helping talkback callers kick their credit habit, the show was a huge success.

While we've always prided the program on its cool tunes, profiles of young Barefoot Entrepreneurs, and that we genuinely have a hell of a lot of fun (mixed in with lame jokes and some occasional coarse language). All that stuff is what makes the show sound good. The thing that gives us our edge is that we get some of the most successful people in the world to talk directly with our fellow Barefooters.

In the early stages I was told that I'd never get guests to go on a student radio. Over the last year we have had the head honchos from many of Australia's biggest listed companies, best-selling authors, some of the best fund managers in the world, not to mention entre- preneurs like Sir Richard Branson, Anita Roddick, Gerry Harvey and Aussie John Symond. Our guests aren't teachers, they're not selling seminars at outrageous prices – they're people who have become the best at what they do and they share it with my audience.

In the finance world people don't take much notice of you until you have some grey hair, which is thought to symbolise experience. I celebrate my youth. I've created something unique using my creativity and passion. I've sacrificed a lot to get *The Barefoot Investor* off the ground, and I wouldn't have it any other way.

I'm treading my own path and in the end, that's what makes me happy.

Website Directory

INTRODUCTION: GOING BAREFOOT

www.barefootinvester.com
The cyber home of the Barefoot Investor. Register on the site for updates, a quarterly newsletter and all things Barefoot.

CHAPTER 1: KEEP IT REAL

The Sunday Times Rich List
www.timesonline.co.uk

CHAPTER 2: LOOKING OUT FOR NUMBER ONE

To compare banks
www.moneysupermarket.co.uk
www.moneyextra.com
www.find.co.uk
http://uk.biz.yahoo.com
www.moneynet.co.uk

Banking disputes
Financial Ombudsman
www.financial-ombudsman.org.uk

General consumer information on banks
British Bankers Association
www.bba.org.uk

Banking Code Standards Board
www.bankingboard.org.uk

Financial Services Authority
www.fsa.gov.uk/consumer

Online Savings Accounts
www.bankofscotlandhalifax.co.uk
www.barclays.co.uk
www.cahoot.com
www.co-operativebank.co.uk
www.firstdirect.com
www.firsttrustbank.co.uk
www.hsbc.co.uk
www.ingdirect.co.uk
www.if.com
www.lloydstsb.com
www.natwest.com
www.smile.co.uk

Bank of England
www.bankofengland.co.uk

CHAPTER 3: REPO YOUR REPAYMENTS

Mobile Phones
www.orange.co.uk
www.o2.co.uk
www.t-mobile.co.uk
www.vodafone.co.uk

Telecommunications ombudsman
www.ortelo.co.uk

Regulator
www.ofcom.org.uk

Student Loans
Department for Education and Skills
www.dfes.gov.uk

Directgov
www.directgov.gov.uk

Student Loan Company
www.slc.co.uk

Credit checking
Callcredit plc
One Park Lane
Leeds
LS3 1EP
Tel. 0113 244 155
www.callcredit.com

Equifax
Capital House
25 Chapel Street
London
NW1 5DS
www.equifax.co.uk

Experian
Talbot House
Talbot Street
Nottingham
NG80 1TH
Tel. 0870 241 6212
www.experian.com

Financial Counselling
www.nationaldebtline.co.uk
www.creditaction.org.uk
www.citizensadvice.org.uk
www.cas.org.uk

CHAPTER 4: WORK YOUR MOJO

General
London Stock Exchange
www.londonstockexchange.com

Independent financial advice
www.unbiased.co.uk

Taxation Office
HM Revenue and Customs
www.hmrc.gov.uk

Financial Services Authority
www.fsa.gov.uk

Fund Supermarkets
Fidelity Funds Network
www.fidelity.co.uk

Interactive Investor
www.iii.co.uk

Fund Information
www.morningstar.com
www.trustnet.com

Ethical Investing
Ethical Investment Association
www.ethicalinvestment.org.uk

Ethical Investment Research Service
www.eiris.org

UK Social Investment Forum
www.uksif.org

Compound Interest Calculator
www.moneymatterstome.co.uk
www.fool.co.uk/school/compound.htm

Authors' websites
www.motivatedmoney.com.au
www.capitalistpig.com

CHAPTER 5: HAVE A BACKUP PLAN

Car and contents insurance
www.cornhilldirect.co.uk
www.directline.com
www.esure.com
www.landg.com
www.autodirectinsuranceservices.co.uk
www.theaa.com
www.morethan.com

Health insurance
www.axa.co.uk
www.bupa.co.uk
www.standardlifehealthcare.co.uk
www.wpa.org.uk

Insurance Comparisons
www.moneynet.co.uk
www.moneysupermarket.com
www.moneyextra.com

Professional Organisations
Chartered Insurance Institute
www.cii.co.uk

Association of British Insurers
www.abi.org.uk

Insurance complaints
www.financial-ombudsman.org.uk

Pensions Regulator
www.thepensionsregulator.gov.uk

Finding lost pension contributions
Department for Work and Pensions
www.dwp.gov.uk

The Pensions Advisory Service
www.opas.org.uk

Pensions Protection Fund
www.ppf.gov.uk

CHAPTER 6: PROPERTY: A BRITISH LOVE AFFAIR

Mortgages
www.abbey.com
www.alliance-leicester.co.uk
www.barclays.co.uk
www.britannia.co.uk
www.cahoot.com
www.co-operativebank.co.uk
www.firstactive.co.uk
www.firstdirect.com
www.halifax.co.uk
www.nationwide.co.uk
www.woolwich.co.uk

Research
FT House Price Index
www.acadametrics.co.uk/ftHousePrice.php

Office of the Deputy Prime Minister
www.opdm.gov.uk

Cheltenham and Gloucester Affordability Index
www.cheltglos.co.uk

Her Majesties Land Registry
www.hmlr.gov.uk

Council of Mortgage Lenders
www.cml.org.uk

FSA
www.fsa.gov.uk/tables

Hometrack
www.hometrack.co.uk

CHAPTER 7: BAREFOOT ENTREPRENEURS

Entrepreneurship
www.business.gov.au
www.ninemsn.com

Barefoot Entrepreneur websites
bloomcosmetics.com.au
www.peteralexander.com.au
www.barefootinvestor.com